Acclaim for Dr. Brandon E. Martin's
LEADING IN THE UNKNOWN

A New Paradigm for Leaders in Intercollegiate Athletics

"Leading in the Unknown is a must read for leaders in college athletics. Dr. Martin offers an excellent road map for leaders in handling student-athletes, coaches, and departmental personnel especially during this precarious period where information has been limited. *Leading in the Unknown* provides a powerful framework and strategies that will enable to leaders to deal with fluidity and change. It is an invaluable resource to have available as we continue to navigate through challenging times."

Joe Castiglione,
Vice President for Intercollegiate Athletics—
University of Oklahoma

Dr. Brandon Martin is one of the rising stars in college athletics. He is a true leader, who isn't just talking about what must be done to create more equity and diversity in the industry, but he's actually a doer. He is offering informed, analytical solutions to complex problems. His leadership will prove invaluable in the coming years as college athletics deals with a changing landscape. This book can serve as a road map for athletic directors and leaders in college athletics and for those who want to affect change.

Andy Katz,
NCAA.com/Turner Sports/
Big Ten Network/Fox Sports.

"Brandon Martin has innovatively aggregated thought-provoking contributors and assembled a very interesting book of useful lessons. Dr. Martin's experiences as a high-level student-athlete combined with an energetic and upwardly mobile set of career achievements make him uniquely positioned to offer insights and ideas that serve leaders in athletics, as well as those in other areas of leadership.

I believe that most readers will find meaningful and helpful applications."

***Bob Bowlsby**,*
Commissioner Big XII Conference

"A timely resource for leaders throughout the college athletics space. This book epitomizes leadership as we approach a new normal in college athletics. A must read!"

***Dennis Dodd**,*
CBS Sports

"Leading in the Unknown is an invaluable resource that all leaders can utilize for guidance in this period of change and uncertainty. Dr. Martin provides a cutting-edge blueprint for decision-making and management during crises and fluidity. This book truly encapsulates a new paradigm for how we as leaders should approach the unknown now and in the future."

***Kathy Nelson**,*
President and CEO
Kansas City Sports Commission

"Brandon Martin has established himself as a progressive and successful servant leader in university administration and college athletics. Dr. Martin provides a critically important resource that will serve many in this challenging and evolving environment. This book is certain to be included on the "must read" list for leaders and administrators throughout higher education."

Mike Alden,
University of Missouri Director
of Athletics (Emeritus)

"Dr Martin's book and its thesis of leadership during uncertain times has doubled up on relevancy. This scholar-practioner's book is timely and timeless. As a former NCAA collegiate athlete, I really respect the credibility that Dr. Martin brings to the landscape of athletics and higher education."

Dr. C. Keith Harrison,
Professor UCF Devos School of Business

"Dr. Martin has identified a critical and timely issue within the landscape of college athletics. The pressure of Athletic Director's, Conference Commissioners, and higher education administrators to make prudent decisions for student-athletes has never been greater. Martin's foresight and timing with "Leading in the Unknown" is impeccable."

Kenneth L. Shropshire
CEO, Global Sport Institute
Adidas Distinguished Professor of Global Sport,
ASU Professor Emeritus, Wharton School

"Change and uncertainty has been ever-present for every coach and administrator during this period. This book serves as a model on how we should identify growth opportunities in crises"

Gary Pinkel,
Missouri Head Football Coach (Emeritus)

Dr. Brandon Martin has dedicated his professional life towards the betterment of young people through college athletics. He has perspectives unique to him as a former student-athlete, athletics administrator, adjunct professor and having served institutions of varying size and scope. Dr. Martin's book will serve as another useful tool for all those involved in leadership roles and college athletics.

Pat Chun, Director of Athletics
—Washington State University

LEADING IN THE UNKNOWN

A NEW PARADIGM FOR LEADERS IN INTERCOLLEGIATE ATHLETICS

By
DR. BRANDON E. MARTIN

COPYRIGHT PAGE

Purpose Publishing
1503 Main Street #168
Grandview, Missouri 64030
www.PurposePublishing.com

Leading in the Unknown: A New Paradigm for Intercollegiate Athletics
Copyright © 2021 Dr. Brandon E. Martin
ISBN:

Book Cover Design: Zac Logsdon, Old Hat Creative
Interior Design: Amit Dey, DeyHouse

All rights reserved. No part of this book may be reproduced by any mechanical, photographic, or electronic process, or in the form of a photographic recording; nor may it be stored in a retrieval system, transmitted, or otherwise be copied for public or private use- other than for "fair use" as brief quotations embodied in articles and reviews-without permission of the publisher.

For information about special discounts for bulk purchases, please contact Dr. Brandon Martin at bmartin53@gmail.com.
Website: docbrandonmartin.com

Printed in the United States of America.

Dedication

To those at the vanguard of equality,
empowerment, and justice.
May your paths be protected by God's hand,
grace, and love.

Acknowledgements

I acknowledge and thank God for the blessings, fortitude, and insights to develop this project. He is my most powerful source of purpose, humility, and fulfillment.

I am forever indebted to so many that have made this book possible. As eloquently expressed by Albert Einstein, "Every day I remind myself that my inner and outer life are based on the labors of other men, living and dead, and that I must exert myself in order to give in the same measure as I have received and am still receiving."

With deep gratitude, I want to thank my wife Rosemary and my three children Germany, Riley, and Brandon for providing me a safe and encouraging space to bring this book to fruition. Thank you for encouraging me through the dark days of minimal resolve.

I want to acknowledge my parents Earl and Eleanor for the profound influence they continue to have in my life. Thank you for supporting my vision for this project. Also, special thanks to my aunt Jimmie who has been an integral supporter of my pursuit of comprehensive excellence.

Special thanks to Purpose Publishing (Michelle Gines and Jason Gines) for your unwavering support throughout this project. I appreciate you believing in my vision and for guiding me through the unknown.

With sincerest appreciation, I want to thank all the leaders within intercollegiate athletics who devoted the time and energy to contribute to this project. Thank you for supporting my dream and goal of positively impacting our industry with this book development.

I want to thank my Chancellor Mauli Agrawal at UMKC for giving me a second shot at purpose, service, and impact. Thank you for providing me the platform on campus to have credibility to produce this book. In that same vein, thank you to the student-athletes, coaches, and staff at Kansas City Athletics that inspired me to write this book. Thank you for your trust!

Lastly, special thanks to the noble men of Kappa Alpha Psi Fraternity Inc. for their steadfast support in completing this project. Thank you for your support in epitomizing a higher level of ACHIEVEMENT.

Table of Contents

Introduction.................................. xxv

Chapter One: Recognizing The Contexts of
    Decision-Making 1

- Foundational Wisdom

- Martin's Leadership Moment

- Principle of Leadership – **Understanding Multidimensional Contexts in Critical Moments**

- Profile of Leadership – **Dr. Edward Scott, Director of Athletics, Morgan State University**

- Principle to Practice – Key Action Items

Chapter Two: Rising To A Decision-Making
              Moment 21

- Foundational Wisdom
- Martin's Leadership Moment
- Principle of Leadership – **Cultural Agility**
- Profile of Leadership – **Dr. Derrick Gragg, Senior Vice President for Inclusion, Education, and Community Engagement NCAA**
- Principle to Practice – Key Action Items

Chapter Three: Adding Value in Every Moment...... 43

- Foundational Wisdom
- Martin's Leadership Moment
- Principle of Leadership – **Catalytic Leadership**
- Profile of Leadership – **Dr. Tamica Smith-Jones, Chief Operating Officer/Kennessaw State University**
- Principle to Practice – Key Action Items

Chapter Four: Building Trust In The Moment........ 65

- Foundational Wisdom

- Martin's Leadership Moment
- Principle of Leadership – **Dynamic Flexibility**
- Profile of Leadership – **Mark Ingram, Associate Vice President/Director of Athletics, University of Alabama-Birmingham**
- Principle to Practice – Key Action Items

Chapter Five: Self-Reflection – Relevance In The Moment. 91

- Foundational Wisdom
- Martin's Leadership Moment
- Principle of Leadership – **Mindful Leadership**
- Profile of Leadership – **Jill Bodensteiner, Director of Athletics/Saint Joseph's University**
- Principle to Practice – Key Action Items

Chapter Six: Social Justice – Empowerment In Every Moment 113

- Foundational Wisdom
- Martin's Leadership Moment
- Principle of Leadership – **Cultural Safety**

- Profile of Leadership – **Patti Phillips, CEO and President Women Leaders in College Sports**
- Principle to Practice – Key Action Items

Chapter Seven: Profiles In Leadership – Timeless Wisdom For All Moments. 133

- Introduction
- Leadership in the Unknown 2020 Interviews with:
  - **Allen Greene, Director of Athletics, Auburn University**
  - **Chris Reynolds, Vice President for Intercollegiate Athletics, Bradley University**
  - **Earl Edwards, Director of Athletics/ University of San Diego**
  - **Tom Douple, Commissioner/Summit League Conference**
  - **Trev Alberts, Vice Chancellor of Athetics/ University of Nebraska Omaha**
  - **David Harris, Director of Athletics/ Northern Iowa University**
  - **Bob Bowlsby, Commissioner, Big XII Conference**

- **Tim Duncan, Vice President of Intercollegiate Athletics/University of New Orleans**

My Concluding Thought.......................... 167

References..................................... 169

About The Author............................... 175

Preface

Leading in the Unknown: A New Paradigm for Leaders in Intercollegiate Athletics presents a new vision of leadership for practitioners, scholars, and leaders within higher education. This book is situated within the unprecedented confluence of the global Covid-19 pandemic, societal injustice, and severe economic depression for which intercollegiate athletics was not immune. Dr. Brandon E. Martin is uniquely positioned within the landscape of intercollegiate athletics as a former Division I Athlete, Vice Chancellor/ Athletics Director at the University of Missouri-Kansas City, Respected Scholar, and Co-Chair of the Black Athletic Director Alliance. This work represents the unique collection of experiences that inform Dr. Martin's approach to leadership that acknowledges current cultural realities and the necessity to reimagine how to engage with athletic programs, institutions, and student-athletes.

Traditional leadership strategies and maxims are infused with culturally relevant principles that address current and future challenges facing the world of intercollegiate athletics. In this book, Dr. Martin invites current leadership voices in intercollegiate athletics to illustrate principles of leadership. The following leadership principles are discussed across the first six chapters: 1) multidimensional contexts; 2) cultural agility; 3) catalytic leadership; 4) dynamic flexibility; 5) mindful leadership; and 6) cultural safety. Each of these chapters end with practical takeaways that provide an initial "game plan" for leaders seeking immediate guidance on how to approach challenges in their respective institutions. In a final chapter, additional intercollegiate athletics leaders are featured to continue the conversation with leaders facing crises on multiple fronts. This book is designed to give current and future leaders new language, practices, and approaches to leadership that can elevate equity, diversity, inclusion, and social justice efforts across all levels of intercollegiate athletics.

Introduction

At no other time throughout my twenty-one years in college athletics administration have I been tested more with remaining true to my core values than 2020. This period of the unknown has brought new meaning to the values I have espoused throughout my professional career. Additionally, I have had to adapt to fluidity, particularly as it relates to performance, outcomes, and operational planning. As a person who is naturally structural, linear, and hyper-deliberate, I have been forced to both anticipate and embrace flexibility. This has been a positive "leap" for me as change and contingency planning have become the norm.

I feel this period of the unknown has deeply cemented my beliefs and fundamental perspectives on leadership. As I contemplate my values of faith, service, gratitude, discovery, and love; I understand how each one has been relentlessly tested. I have an even clearer understanding of how powerful God (my higher power) is and the importance of submitting to His model of leading and serving. I lean on his words in Isaiah 41:10, "So do not fear, for I am with you; do not be dismayed, for I am your God. I will strengthen you and help you; I will uphold you with my righteous right hand." In this time of fluidity, transition, and revelation, I know that I must go beyond my own understanding and know that God will equip me with strength, wisdom, and fortitude to combat the unknown. One must have a vision of their preferred leadership style. To this end, it is not the moment that defines you as much as it is the moment defining your true self.

My intent in this book is to share the peaks and valleys of my career in leadership to underscore my experienced disappointment, embarrassment, and greatest of all, humility. Regardless of the predicament, trust in my ability to lead has always been the foundation that has sustained me across several vital roles. As a husband, father, mentor, and especially now as the Vice Chancellor/Director of Athletics at the University of Missouri–Kansas City, this confidence originates from facing and overcoming several challenges that forced me to evolve as a leader.

The payoff for the labor invested came to fruition when I had to make the exceedingly difficult decision that the Kansas City Roos men's basketball team would not travel to Seattle for the scheduled contest against the Seattle Redhawks during a declared global pandemic. The fact that ten of eleven deaths reported at the hands of the coronavirus were in state of Washington may have made the decision look easy. However, in the defining moment, I was forced to evaluate the impact of my student-athletes, the communication to our stakeholders, as well as the long-lasting impact on our donors, season ticket holders, and fans. At the time of writing of this book, the full spectrum of implications is still unknown. I believe that it was the trust I had cultivated with my chancellor and university leadership that gave me the courage necessary amid uncertain circumstances. The ability to be decisive without knowing all the factors has been developed over the years by building a kind of instinctual leadership that allows trust to be built between myself and my team. In this way, my senior executive team was able to reflect trust back to me which empowered me to effectively lead in the midst of indefinite times.

While my journey as a leader is still evolving, I have come to recognize six key traits that have sustained me for more than twenty-one years of practice. It is my goal to share with readers how to use these role defining characteristics to lead in a post COVID-19 world and beyond:

1. Recognizing the Context of Decision-Making
2. Rising to A Decision-Making Moment
3. Adding Value in Every Moment
4. Building Trust in the Moment
5. Self-Reflection: Relevance in the Moment
6. Social Justice: Empowerment in Every Moment.

Each unit will include a case study identifying a designated leader demonstrating how he or she used one, if not all six key traits in times of the unknown. Each case study is designed to help you understand how the engagement of these traits will sustain your leadership mobility throughout your individual career paths. It is my goal to share with readers how to use these role defining traits to lead with a new paradigm for collegiate athletics.

An additional feature is the inclusion of Chapter 7 which is comprised of interviews of featured leaders who faced a myriad of challenges since the beginning of the global COVID-19 pandemic. These prolific leaders in the world of collegiate athletics were interviewed in real-time. Each featured administrator will speak to the intrinsic difficulties of leadership given the cascading events that changed our lives on a local, national, and global level. The interviews are personal, introspective, and insightful. Our selected leaders' responses to several questions will provide important perspectives that can add to your decision-making considerations as we continue to lead into the unknown.

The contextual backdrop for interviews was fluid as societal pressures mounted over the months of the pandemic. As a result, the interviews became more in-depth, and necessarily needed to address a wider range of topics. Chapter 7 will begin with two such expanded interviews that will reflect the reality of escalating issues we all faced with the onset of the pandemic and continued fight for social justice. A key principle I maintain is having a wide array of key voices to help me gain diverse perspectives, thus expanding the context of what is considered in critical moments. It is my hope that you will benefit from the leaders selected for the feature profiles.

Let us begin our journey in gaining greater clarity for leading in the unknown…

CHAPTER ONE

Recognizing the Contexts of Decision Making

"One of the great ironies in life is that if you give up your life, you gain it. If you help others, you benefit. If you lose yourself, you find yourself."

John C. Maxwell,
Intentional Living: Choosing a Life That Matters

FOUNDATIONAL WISDOM

In this chapter, you will learn through my personal experiences and other prominent athletic administrators how to better understand the contextual realities of defining moments, especially when leading in the unknown. The ability to quickly ascertain the facts and realities of a given crises are critical when determining how to provide leadership. Chip and Dan Heath (2019) stated in their book, *The Power of Moments*, "Defining moments in our lives can never be planned but are ever present in our lives and often burned into our memory, regardless of how or when they happen." This quote leads me to two foundational leadership lessons. First, our defining moments create a leadership blueprint that will become the basis for future decision-making. Second, our ability to quickly ascertain the multiple dimensions in every decision-making context is critical and will help us examine traits for the entirety of the book.

LEADERSHIP MOMENT

My entire athletic career served as the training ground of who I am today. Integrity and purpose have always been key steps throughout my leadership journey. When on the basketball court, I purposed to lead by example. As a program coordinator, committee member or chair, integrity was always at the forefront of my actions and responsibilities. Every opportunity I was given throughout every stage of my development as a leader was a defining moment. This first trait of recognizing defining moments does not begin when you are given a title. It is a trait that remains on a continuum in every area of your life—in every moment you live. To situate this, and the many lessons of the book, let us dig deeper into my origins as a leader.

Like many men throughout the United States, I grew up the son of divorce, with parents committed to strongly co-parenting and being present in my life. My father was a hard-working man who spent long, arduous hours in transportation for the *Los Angeles Times*. My mother was a woman with a beautiful spirit and always wanted me to have a better upbringing than she had growing up in Los Angeles during the civil rights era. My parents remained committed to my education and development even after they divorced when I was 8 years old. Growing up, there were several situations that revealed that I thought well beyond my years. As is often the case, I saw myself through the lens of key adults in my life who had unconventional occupations and interests. I believe it was because I spent a great deal of time with my father and always found myself emerged in the conversations with him and his friends. They would always discuss the various aspects of "the struggle" and how they were paving the way for future generations. One of my father's favorite sayings to me was, "Nobody loves you out here. You have to go out and get it on your own. You don't have any days off as a Black man."

While not a financially wealthy man, my dad regularly sacrificed hundreds of dollars for me to attend some of the most prestigious basketball camps. This sacrifice provided me with a foundational lesson in understanding different aspects of "prosperity." My father had a vision worth sacrificing financially for, to produce a "prosperous" future for me. It is only now that I understand that against the advice of many of his friends and family, he saw each opportunity as a chance to invest in his own legacy. In this lesson, I learned that in the face of an uncertain future, having a vision is its own form of wealth.

I distinctly remember while away at a week-long basketball camp in Santa Barbara, CA when I finally understood what my father meant by, "going out and getting my own." It was in that moment of independence and self-reliance, where I decided what role I wanted basketball to play in my life. It would be much later in my athletic career before I understood how to strategically leverage all those experiences into academic success. As I learned as a child through my father and his friends, effective leadership can only be learned through the lens of others. We need others to reflect to us what they are experiencing to define leadership practices that truly have a lasting impact.

UNDERSTANDING MULTIDIMENSIONAL CONTEXTS IN CRITICAL MOMENTS

In today's world, single cause reasons for social problems or leadership failures are rare, if not impossible. Causal factors are often like putting a hand in a bucket of water. The water ripples out in all directions and then returns to re-cover the hand. The hand becomes submerged by the water, but it is difficult to know what part of the water caused the hand to be submerged. When considering leading in the unknown, the complexities of problems we face may come in like a flood and make it difficult to identify the causal sources. One way to approach complex issues and causes is to have a framework that can identify multiple sources concurrently. It is important to recognize in today's world that we have multiple identities that need consideration when making critical decisions in leadership. As a result, we need to be able to understand that each of these identities have the potential to impact how we lead, especially when so much is unknown. In this book, we are going to frame each chapter using the bio-ecological model of human development. Complex and unknown times require a strong way to consider issues at multiple levels to anticipate consequences more accurately from decisions made when so much is ambiguous or unfamiliar.

Since leadership involves multiple components of one's characteristics and values, it is important to recognize that there are multiple dimensions in need of consideration when making critical decisions. Each component of these identities has the potential to impact how we lead, particularly when so much of what is to come is unknown. Throughout this book, I am going to utilize Bronfenbrenner's bioecological model of human development (which addresses multiple dimensions of human development) as a fundamental foundation outlining the complexity of a leader's make-up. Being familiar with this model will help you, the emerging leader, to evaluate and embrace the complexity of today's issues, at multiple levels, in order to more accurately anticipate the consequences of decisions made (Krebs, 2009).

Recognizing the Contexts of Decision Making 9

Bronfenbrenner's Bioecological Model of Human Development

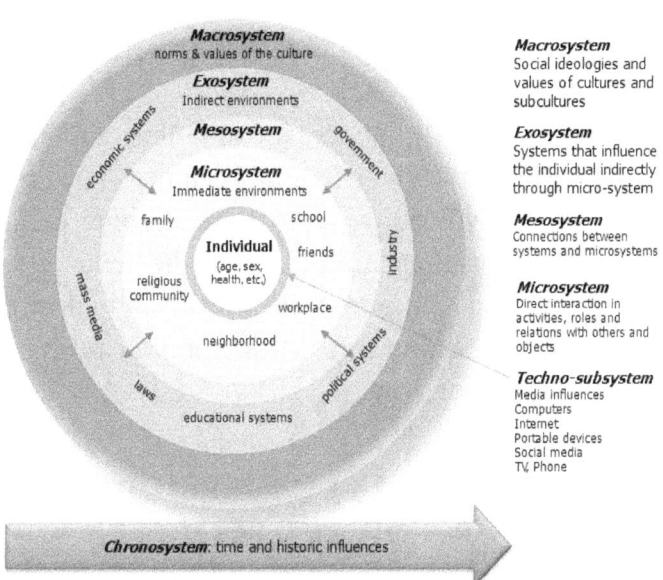

(http://drewlichtenberger.com/6-shaping-influences-human-development/)

While each level of Brofrenbrenner's model is important, three are primarily featured in this book, the *Individual/Microsystem* (these will be treated interchangeably in the book), *Exosystem*, and *Macrosystem* levels. The *Individual/Microsystem* level looks at characteristics such as age, sex, and health. As technology has advanced and become almost as important as our biological systems, the *Individual* level extends to the *Techno-subsystem* level which includes media influences, computers, internet, portable devices, television, and phones. The *Exo-system* level will allow us to look at some of the interrelated systems in society, higher education, and athletics. The *Macrosystem* level will allow us to examine the cultural realities that are causing so much of the unknowns.

PROFILE OF LEADERSHIP – DR. EDWARD SCOTT

It is one thing for us to discuss, examine, and analyze each of the six leadership traits outlined in this book. However, I believe it will best serve you to understand how the application of these traits position you to come out on the other side of the unknown a much wiser leader as a result of the experience, regardless of the time or place. Bill

George (2009), author of *7 Lessons for Leading in Crisis*, wrote, "Even when leaders acknowledge their responsibility, they may face significant resistance from their organizations in solving a (crisis) because people have great difficulty in admitting their mistakes. This is why crises require so much skill on the leader's part." This enlightening statement is one of many key revelations George highlights in the first lesson for leading in crisis: Face Reality, Starting with Self.

Case Study: Dr. Edward Scott, Athletic Director, Morgan State University

- Dr. Edward Scott, Director of Intercollegiate Athletics
- Morgan State University (2016) - Baltimore, MD
- More than 17 years in athletic administration. Dr. Scott oversees the department's 14 Division I programs with nearly 300 student-athletes who compete for Mid-Eastern Athletic Conference (MEAC) and NCAA

championships. In addition to handling the department's day-to-day operations, Dr. Scott reports directly to President Dr. David Wilson and is the first Athletics director to hold a seat on the President's Cabinet.

Defining Moment

I was 23 years old and had just finished playing professional baseball. It was my first year as Assistant Director of Student-Athlete Support Services. I was trying to figure out if working in athletics was a career or a job for the time being. I realized early on that it (college athletics) was a lifestyle. I actively sought career advice, but found during my search, I had acquired a gift for foresight and the ability to motivate others with a desire for personal improvement. I noticed that my former teammates and peer athletes began to gravitate toward me, seeking my insight and often following my advice. As I began to embrace my leadership role as assistant director, I found my students were increasingly coming back looking for my advice and guidance. I was surprised at the way they relied on me. This was the first time I knew I was making an immediate, positive impact on people who relied on my leadership. This was the defining moment when I knew athletics was a career for me, not a job. The intrinsic value that I derive from helping people (older and younger) achieve their goals through sports is a powerful feeling that I thoroughly enjoy. I am competitive; I learned early on that working in athletics allows me to fulfill my competitive need, while serving student-athletes, coaches, and staff.

Decision Making

Less than six months into my position as Associate Athletics Director for Student Services, I learned that one of our most talented student-athletes did not pass the required six credit hours needed for our post-season competition. I was the only administrator aware of this discrepancy and had the weight of revealing this moment altering information at the cost of the university and my integrity as leader. In this moment, there were more mitigating factors than most people can understand. This athlete was the only African American on the team and I was the only African American administrator. While the decision seemed simple–he did not acquire the six credit hours needed to compete, so he does not qualify to play–the implications of this decision would resonate on two quite different levels in two vastly different environments. I had to decide between doing what was right and winning.

Adding Value/Building Trust

Trust takes time to build and can be solidified during a crisis. I have built trust with staff and coaches by being extremely transparent in my approach to making decisions. I must be very authentic and vulnerable as a leader during those pivotal moments that have the potential to change people's lives and show the human side of leadership. Timing and communication also play an essential role when leading in the unknown. Trust and the conveyed value of those I am responsible to lead are necessary to make sure my team feels informed and empowered to make decisions on their level.

Self-Care

Self-care is established by maintaining balance in the areas that have proven most valuable to me. 2020 and the world pandemic required me to expand my approach to communicating with those I work with by adapting to utilizing our virtual space since I could no longer walk around to randomly see people. I have learned that scheduling more meetings for shorter periods of time has proven to be effective. I schedule athletic executive meetings following my president's cabinet meeting to ensure the team gets the most current updates from the highest level which has been helpful in maintaining alignment with the larger university.

My family continues to be a vital component of who I am as a leader, therefore I ensure I preserve a routine that provides balance and consistency regardless of the unknown. I work out every morning, and reserve time for my family after dinner to put our daughter to bed. I dedicate a minimum of 30-minutes for reading per night, followed by an hour of uninterrupted time with my wife.

PRINCIPLE TO PRACTICE – KEY ACTION ITEMS

Dr. Scott's case study provides many examples of how the bioecological model can be a powerful way to understand how simultaneous factors can influence defining moments that become the blueprint for how we lead. For example, when considering reporting a student-athlete to administration Dr. Scott states, "The implications of this decision would resonate on two quite different levels in two vastly different environments. I had to make a decision between doing what was right and winning." Beyond just being an ethical issue, Dr. Scott teaches us by context that at the time, both he and the student-athlete were the only African Americans in the situation. When looking at the model below, we see that consideration illuminates all the dimensions activated in that defining moment. I will use the model below to illustrate the multidimensional aspects of this critical moment.

Dr. Scott allows us to see that considerations of the *Microsystem* level are critical in understanding the difficult decision before him. The immediate environment of Dr. Scott's *Microsystem* level revealed that at a group level, he and the student-athlete were in an extreme minority by race. Additional dynamics such as workplace environment and culture, administrative precedent, and fallout from the student-athlete's family and friends are all critical contextual factors to be considered when making defining decisions. The bioecological model provides a framework to consider these factors in "real time." Another critical contextual factor is the interplay between institutions of higher learning at the *Exosystem* level with the multiple dimensions at the *Microsystem* level. A potential reality is that African American culture is not fully understood by *Exosystem* level influences, and as such often places leaders of color in positions where leadership is challenged.

In a single decision which should have been simple, Dr. Scott struggled with the fact his choice to deny this student-athlete the opportunity to play in a championship gam, because he valued that every component of his *Microsystem* had the potential to sabotage the very components of this African American student-athlete's *Ecosystem* level, which should have complimented each other.

Most cultures of color place high value on education, because it is the one intangible thing that validates prosperity beyond the economic system. However, in the predominately white culture, education confirms the validity to one's right to pursue all the riches the economic systems have to offer. Regardless of culture or race, most athletes struggle with what to sacrifice to be superior. However, it often comes down to how great of a penalty will be paid when that sacrifice is used to define the athlete in totality. Under normal circumstances, this situation should have served as a lesson on which sacrifices matter the most. However, because he was the only African American player on the team, his failure more than likely served as a stereotype and confirmation of what is assumed about most athletes of color–smart enough to play, but not smart enough to excel academically. Dr. Scott, a former student-athlete of color himself, understood the ramifications of his decision.

Bill George's second lesson for leading in crisis is: Do Not Be Atlas; Get the World Off Your Shoulders. In this instance, Dr. Scott found himself struggling with the desire to protect the reputation of an entire race while grappling with his own competitiveness and an opportunity to bolster the university's odds of winning a championship. By ridding himself of all that extra baggage, Dr. Scott was able to lead with integrity and his commitment to the student and the athlete.

Key Takeaways

- Bioecological model has the capacity to give leaders multiple perspectives when making critical decisions in defining moments.
- Defining moments create decision-making blueprints that will shape what critical determinations are considered as we lead in the unknown.
- The unknown can be mitigated by honestly addressing cultural factors that heavily influence both leaders and those impacted by decisions.

CHAPTER TWO

Advancing to a Decision-Making Moment

> "Every problem introduces a person to himself. Each time we encounter a painful experience, we get to know ourselves a little better."
>
> John C. Maxwell, *The 15 Invaluable Laws of Growth*

FOUNDATIONAL WISDOM

Roman general and politician, Julius Caesar, is well-known for the axiom "experience is the best teacher." Our decisions in life are often influenced by experiences we have encountered. Years ago, as a basketball student-athlete, I made decisions to shift right or left pending on how my opponent defended. In retrospect, I was totally dependent on skill and the "known"—familiarity was my ally. However, as an administrator, I found *familiarity* should only be used as a guide. I learned the hard way that comfort, which is often the by-product of the familiar, can be dangerous when leading in the unknown.

If you have ever found yourself searching for the light switch in a dark room that was once occupied by small children with toys, you quickly come to realize that the only fact you can rely on is knowing exactly where the light switch is located. Each step requires preparedness for the possibility of an unknown encounter, yet you know that your ability to reach that switch is the only way you will clearly see what the situation truly looks like. Such is the journey of a leader in the unknown. Your decision-making abilities are intended to rectify the issue at hand, but very often that decision also reveals unexpected challenges you did not see coming.

It is critically important to remember that *every* decision you make as a leader must be done with the intent of the greater good. Nothing good can ever come of rising to the occasion with anything else. Good or bad, every decision comes with a consequence—the result of an action. Through my shared experience at a large, western region state university, you will learn how to apply internal and external influences to guide your decision-making traits.

MARTIN'S LEADERSHIP MOMENT

One's title serves as a summary of expectations. As the Director of Athletics at a large western state institution, I was expected to lead in university relations, design and support operation plans supporting university goals, and many other duties and responsibilities all while building trusting relationships with my staff. When you spend quality time with those you work with, you tend to build camaraderie as you become familiar with their family and friends, as well as their preferences and idiosyncrasies.

After welcoming an accomplished and celebrated coach as the institution's Head Men's Basketball Coach in 2013, I began building that necessary relationship for success. With a common thread in basketball, the new coach and I exchanged childhood stories and found that we shared familiar community values and background experiences. Like many other staff members, I built a familiarity with the coach, his team, and his family. Unfortunately, after a 53-105 record following five seasons with the institution and the men's basketball team finishing last in the conference in three of our last four seasons during his tenure, it was decided to move in a different direction as a program.

I committed to embrace this decision-making moment, because I was familiar with the process of acting in the best interest of the university, student-athletes, and athletics program. As stressful as it may be, hiring and firing comes with this leadership position. However, this was the first time I found myself entangled in a cultural context where the similitude of backgrounds introduced unique dynamics which blurred the lines between personal and professional considerations. As a result, I temporarily lost sight of my purpose as a leader in this moment of the unknown. An invaluable point of consideration I learned is that familiarity in leadership should only be used as a tool. Understanding the lines between personal and professional contexts can bring clarity of action in the realm of the unknown. Having the cultural agility to avoid disastrous outcomes can transform decision-making in critical decision-making moments.

As I entered the conference room, I quickly surmised that my soon to be terminated coach was ready to refute any reasons to let him go. While any termination meeting can be filled with tension and anxiety, this moment quickly transitioned from the professional realm to a personal character attack that took me to a mental place of protection and survival. In the moment my coach stood to challenge my decision from a personal and familiar perspective. My surroundings were transformed from the leadership role I played to the person protecting his character and manhood at all costs. This was the first time a staff member ever challenged me with words and a posture on such a personal level that it required a culturally engrained response. I found myself later struggling with my response as man who rose to the moment of expected reaction, rather than the leader who should have risen above the familiar and into the developing moment of the unknown. I made the wrong decision for what I thought was the right reason. That decision-making moment became about me personally (my ego), not the transformative and respected leader that I had been at the institution.

PRINCIPLE OF LEADERSHIP: CULTURAL AGILITY

The complexity of the leadership moment presented above will require some disentangling to extract the full potential for learning the key principle of cultural agility. First, Caligiuri and Lundby (2014) define cultural agility as the "ability to quickly, comfortably and effectively work in different cultures and with people from different cultures." Further, "culturally agile leaders are able to correctly read the cross-cultural or multicultural context and respond appropriately—whether to adapt to a cultural difference and comport one's behaviors to the host nationals' expectations, to override cultural differences and behave in a manner that is consistent with an organizational standard, or to integrate multiple cultural differences and create a new approach" (Caligiuri & Lundby, 2014). As a result, culturally agile leaders can quickly absorb contextual factors, understand multidimensional realities, and pivot in culturally appropriate ways that match expectations across all environments.

As mentioned in the previous chapter, we must first understand the cultural context of the moment to better describe the multiple elements present that lead to the outcome. First, the coach who was being terminated and I grew up in remarkably similar ways. In fact, geographically we both experienced socialization in Southcentral Los Angeles, which taught us to be tough and respond with force to all challenges of our manhood. We both had used athletics to navigate perilous environments and overcome limitations of what many of our peers fell victim to in and around our neighborhoods. We both had ascended to positions in our post athletic careers that required navigating environments where we were often in the minority compared with our colleagues. With hindsight, I can see the level of semblance that brought us to our moment of conflict. It is in this spirit of honest self-reflection where I would like to explicate how being more culturally agile could have shifted the dynamics of the moment.

The multiple dimensions impacting the leadership moment are important to understand how cultural agility could have mitigated the circumstances leading to an undesirable outcome. The contextual factors of having two African American men with extremely similar backgrounds holding high profile positions within the higher education space is key. Expectations of cultural agility to "behave in a manner that is consistent with an organizational standard," is squarely situated within one's ability to assess the cultural environment setting behavioral rules. Key questions to be considered are:

1. Are the rules the same by race, gender, sexual orientation, etc.?
2. Who (by race, gender, sexual orientation, etc.) gets to enforce the behavioral rules in the institution or organization?
3. What are the differential consequences (by race, gender, sexual orientation, etc.) for breaking the rules?

These critical queries are hugely important for leaders looking to act ethically and equitably in defining moments of leadership. The moment described above had clear answers to these queries that lead to the eventual outcome based on the dimensional interaction between the *Exosystem* (i.e., educational system) and the *Microsystem* (i.e., African American men) levels. However, I understand that an adherence to cultural agility could have shifted the outcome. Let us explore how I could have pivoted in this decisive moment.

Cultural agility should lead to a new approach that considers contextual factors and multidimensional realities. The culturally agile leader understands that each contextual factor and reality in the moment is going to exert pressure on what needs to be considered in decisive moments. In many cases, environmental inputs will trigger responses based on how we have been socialized to respond when placed in certain situations. In my case, I was triggered and needed to display greater cultural agility in recognition of the expected behavioral comportment expected at my level of leadership. Further, the cultural context dictated that the likelihood that anyone in the education system would understand the cultural context of my response was extremely low. I have since moved on to a new awareness of cultural agility that has better enabled me to lead into the unknown.

Culturally agile leadership has the capacity to prepare programs and institutions to have more equitable perspectives. This is especially true when there are different cultural perspectives to consider in an intercultural exchange. The intercultural interactions between the coach and I contained several perspectives that required a sophisticated cultural lens to fully understand what happened in the exchange. The cultural agility framework can impact the interpretive lens that one uses to understand complex situations. The unknown is often replete with complex and difficult options that include considering multiple cultural perspectives at any given time. We will see this complexity demonstrated in the following profile of leadership of Dr. Derrick Gragg.

PROFILE OF LEADERSHIP – DR. DERRICK GRAGG

In their book, *Learning Leadership: The Five Fundamentals of Becoming an Exemplary Leader*, James

Kouzes and Barry Posner (2016) wrote, "Learning to be the best leader you can requires you to be clear about what you value and what you care enough about to be willing to make sacrifice." Determinates of sacrifice are often based on context, perspective, and perceived consequences. The context is vital in understanding all the constituent elements that need to be considered in decisive moments. Once context is considered, determinations can be made about to what degree things are being given up and who is sacrificing the most in each situation. Lastly, willingness to make sacrifices infers that one has done a deep analysis of potential consequences that will likely shift outcomes for both the leader and those being led. It is with this understanding that we engage our next profile in leadership.

Embarking on his newest journey into the unknown as newly appointed NCAA Senior Vice President of Inclusion, Education and Community Engagement, Dr. Derrick Gragg is reminded of the 23-year-old version of himself beginning his athletic career as an Academic Counselor at his Alma Mater, Vanderbilt University. Having just left a one-year stint in law school, Gragg was working full-time guiding and counseling incoming student-athletes. After wrapping up a 45-minute presentation to a group of prospective students, Gragg recalls his supervisor turning to him to say, "Next week you are going to start doing these presentations, because you will be better at this than me. Those guys will relate to you because you have lived their experience in many ways." Gragg remembers that as a "big moment of clarity" for him. Gragg realized in that moment it was not just his former ability on the football field that made him the best person for the job, nor was it his gift for public speaking and communication; but it was his commitment to his core values of respect, integrity, passion, collegiality, and teamwork that drove every leadership decision he had made.

Case Study: Dr. Derrick Gragg, NCAA Senior Vice President of Inclusion, Education and Community Engagement

- Dr. Derrick Gragg, Former Vice President and Director of Athletics at University of Tulsa

- Vanderbilt University (1992) – Nashville, Tennessee
- During more than 27 years as an intercollegiate athletics administrator, Dr. Gragg has built a professional athletic administrative career as a Director of Athletics with one of the longest tenures ever held at Eastern Michigan University, and later as the Vice President and Director of Athletics at University of Tulsa.

Defining Moment

My pivotal decision-making moment came when I was a Director of Athletics faced with the choice of terminating a successful, long-time, popular coach for violating professional ethical standards. As a leader, I consistently remind coaches and staff members that our decision-making processes must be student-athlete centric, meaning that we make decisions that support the best interests of the student-athletes, rather than ourselves and our careers. In this instance, it was clear that the coach's actions warranted his release and any effort to retain him would have positioned the university to face extreme backlash from the student-athletes we were committed to supporting and the parents who had placed their trust in our ability to lead by example.

Decision Making

One can sometimes find oneself walking a tight rope between their core values and what is popular. However, I have learned that when faced with the decision of doing what may seem to be popular at the moment, it is always best to lean toward the constant support of your core values regardless of the potential outcome. Time and events have always proven that popularity fades with the moment, while core values have and always withstand the test of time. I found myself resisting the challenge of teetering on this quandary while holding steadfast under the extreme, external pressure of a chair on the board of trustees, who was a close friend of the coach in question. In addition to violating the ethical standards, the coach had also violated NCAA rules and regulations. Unfortunately, the chair sought to protect his friend rather than stand by my decision and support the student-athletes.

Adding Value/Building Trust

Understanding the risk, I chose to maintain the trust of our university team and the impacted student-athlete and his family by moving forward with the termination. Trust is always at the center of any effective relationship. I have gained and maintained the trust of staff throughout my career, never just in a moment. I have accomplished this by always being truthful, transparent, and honest (brutally honest at times, but it is better than dodging or avoiding issues that need to be addressed for the good of the organization).

Self-Care

Perspective is the key. As an athlete you learn quickly that losing is a part of playing the game. As a leader you come to realize that loss will be a part of your experience at the helm and like any loss it remains a part of your leadership make up. However, it is the lesson you choose to carry with you that prepares you for the unknown. I am reminded of my first year playing football as a 7-year-old boy. We had lost a game during the season and many of my team members cried afterwards. As tears began to well up in my eyes, my mother said very strongly, "No! We do not cry when we lose games! Dry it up!"

With the mentality of loss as an opportunity to learn and "next-time" as a gift to do better established in my psyche, I tend to move past losses very quickly, even heartbreaking losses like all leaders experience. I instead like to focus and dwell on victories and great milestones, rather than negative moments. As such, I have developed a mental discipline that allows me to stay true to my core ethics, while maintaining a healthy sense of self. Leadership, in this way, is not about being perfect and ignoring losses. Rather, leadership is about a resetting of the mind when negative moments occur back towards a winning mindset that can propel an organization forward.

PRINCIPLE TO PRACTICE – KEY ACTION ITEMS

This case demonstrates multiple elements of cultural agility. Dr. Gragg was placed in a situation where his cultural ethics were challenged by other environmental forces that were being driven by different cultural ethics. Dr. Gragg's core cultural values are respect, integrity, passion, collegiality, and teamwork that infused his thinking around decision-making in critical moments. Values are not created in a vacuum and often are laden with cultural socialization that we receive across our entire lives. In short, our values come from somewhere and are often taught to us by someone. In this way, we can understand that Dr. Gragg had to employ cultural agility to come to an important decision where he was certainly acting in the best interest of student-athletes, the program, and his institution. Each of these constituents were considered in his decision-making process. Choosing his core cultural values over the loyalty being shown between two friends certainly involved an analysis of potential sacrifices that may have impacted his personal leadership journey. Dr. Gragg proved to be a culturally agile leader, while staying true to his core values.

Cultural agility in leadership is an essential skill that is needed for leading into the unknown. When difficult and complex situations arise, it will be the culturally agile leader who will have the skillset to analyze the context, understand the cultural realities of the moment, and decisively move forward. Caligiuri and Lundy (2014) found that cultural agility was needed throughout organizations, but that the tone needs to be set from the top. The responsibility of ingratiating these principles is the responsibility of senior leadership who will consistently adhere to a set of culturally relevant ideas that best fit the environmental context. As such, cultural agility will become a core value in any program or institution where successful outcomes are sought that consider various cultural perspectives.

Key Takeaways

- Culturally agile leaders can quickly absorb contextual factors that aide in ethical and equitable decision-making.
- Culturally agile leaders understand multidimensional realities that consider diversity, equity, and inclusion of all involved.
- Culturally agile leaders pivot in culturally appropriate ways that match expectations across all environments.

CHAPTER THREE

Adding Value in Every Moment

"Remember, the role of leadership is to serve, that is, to identify and meet legitimate needs. In the process of meeting needs, we will often be called upon to make sacrifices for those we serve."

James C. Hunter, *The Servant: A Simple Story About the True Essence of Leadership*

FOUNDATIONAL WISDOM

Learning evaluation skills is a core responsibility for every emerging leader as they develop across a career trajectory. Central to the task of evaluation is teasing out how to effectively set metrics for how valuable an entity is at critical key decision-making moments. Determining values, becomes central to understanding both the process and desired outcomes of leadership. For example, building value in the moment is much like increasing the currency return on a dated nickel–it is the collector who can truly grasp and appreciate how much it's actually worth. Our contextual world often presents circumstances that augment how, and to what degree, our values change after salient experiences that impact who we are in the moment. Further, this value determination greatly impacts who we become as leaders.

Upon critical reflection after transitioning from a large western state institution, I began to question my personal values in every facet of life. Namely, my career, family, and ability to contribute as the respected leader I worked so hard to become. In moments of deep reflection, I found myself questioning key decisions that occurred in my Athletic Director role and identity. This reflection led to the crystallization of an action I have come to highly value, which is taking a step away to regroup, reassess, and reevaluate myself holistically. Taking time to evaluate one's values is indeed an invaluable gift that, in this case, came at a critical time in my career journey. With the benefit of time, comes the inevitable wisdom of understanding of truly how important values are in pivotal decision-making moments.

Typically, I am one who believes that life offers a finite number of chances to succeed, therefore it is our obligation to take advantage of each opportunity presented to us. In a moment where I was reeling from a chance to succeed as an Athletic Director, I needed an opportunity to present itself. I was invited to join my friend and colleague Mike

Thorne to become President and CEO of a 501c3 organization he founded in 2017, Home Field 4 Champions. The non-profit organization was established to provide academic, sport, and leadership service through athletic programming to adolescent and teenage youth in the Greater Los Angeles area. In this case, Mike was the evaluator who never stopped seeing the value in my abilities as a leader.

In this value-added moment, I learned through humility to embrace my "whole" self. In this moment, I gained so much through the opportunity to impact so many students' lives. As a result, I became a better spouse, a stronger advocate for my son's interests and passions, and established a closer bond with my daughters. When you allow yourself to add value in every moment, you in turn learn more about yourself and have a greater appreciation for those people who matter most.

MARTIN'S LEADERSHIP MOMENT

Having served in a role where I had a large staff ready to execute a robust work portfolio, I had to make significant adjustments to my leadership disposition. I was given stewardship over four full time staff members and five part time members to serve approximately 210 youth participants who were convinced they had the makings of a multi-million-dollar athlete waiting to be discovered. I found myself needing to adapt to a new culture where I had to prove myself all over again. This was a great opportunity to rediscover that strong core values work regardless of the size and scale of the organization. In truth, I was reinvigorated as a leader, and took seriously the task of ensuring that I fulfilled my charge.

I quickly realized that to add value to this moment, I needed to engage three specific leadership elements – worth, wisdom, and empowerment. I had to prove to this staff that beyond all the athletic accolades, I was worthy of this position. I needed to show my staff that as president and CEO, I was about the community, not personal gain. I had to demonstrate that I not only understood the business strategy, but that I was willing and able to make those feel-good investments like an "ice cream day" to remind them and our participants that there were rewards for working hard and staying true to the mission. Finally, I had to empower my staff to become just as valuable in their daily decision-making opportunities as our board members were in deciding our ongoing footprint in the community we were serving.

As I took time to invest in this new opportunity, I found myself getting back to the core of who I was as a leader. I relished rolling up my sleeves and working hard with our participants as well as watching parents walk away with the confidence that we were caring for their children just as we would care for our own. It was both liberating and solidifying for me. It was in this moment I found myself more confident that ever that I had what it took to succeed as a leader regardless of my title. I was adding value to my character in preparation to get back to the journey of my destiny.

PRINCIPLE OF LEADERSHIP – CATALYTIC LEADESHIP

Leading into the unknown requires a strong commitment to core values and character traits that become the foundational blueprint to engage complex and difficult moments. In this way, leadership equally focuses on the process as much as the outcomes. The phrase "ill-gotten gain" comes to mind when thinking about an outcome that is arrived at through negative means. Further, I contend that positive outcomes resultant from negative processes are not repeatable, bad habit forming, and morally indefensible when placed under scrutiny. The catalytic leader understands that the *how* of leading is as important as *what* is done to get results. Catalytic leaders are well versed in "convening and joining with a diverse group of individuals, forging sustainable agreements, setting into motion multiple strategies, and sustaining momentum over time" (Luke, 1998). The character of a catalytic leader is forged in critical moments that shape how core values will be utilized to accomplish these aforementioned tasks.

Merriam-Webster defines catalyst as "an agent that provokes or speeds significant change or action." This definition positions catalytic leadership as having the capacity to significantly shift dynamics in critical leadership moments. According to Luke (1998) there are three foundational characteristics that distinguish strong catalytic leadership:

1. A continuous focus on desired results
2. A sense of connectedness and relatedness
3. Exemplary personal integrity

As I transitioned from an Athletic Director to CEO of a non-profit, a necessary shift in core priorities took place. The shift in my *Exosystem* level (i.e., education system to public service) awakened my understanding of catalytic leadership. I was thrust into a situation where previous work modalities and ways of leading were tested and in need of transformation to lead in a new context.

The first foundational characteristic, a continuous focus on desired results, meant that I had to internally shift my career clock when the sudden change occurred from Athletics Director to CEO of a non-profit. I had a laser focus on fulfilling my duties as Athletics Director, thus proving my ability to lead at a large western university. The shift in roles allowed me to see that while the context and scope of leadership changed, the core values and principles I had employed to get to that point did not. I had to consider that with a greatly reduced staff and role purview my perspectives had to shift from traditional structures of leadership to a more catalytic model that focused on empowerment, communication, and collaboration. While these were already core values in my leadership portfolio, the infusion of them towards desired results were greatly strengthened because of the transition.

The second foundational characteristic, a sense of connectedness and relatedness, was central to providing catalytic leadership to all the constituent groups within the non-profit. Full and part time employees, parents, and most importantly over 200 youth, were all in need of various touchpoints that would demonstrate my commitment to each of them. Early in the transition, I was able to listen to the needs, desires, and challenges of each of the groups to better grasp what successful outcomes meant to them. As a catalytic leader, it was then up to me to determine how to build an infrastructure that promoted collaboration and trust rather than unidirectional commands and coercion. I understood that sharing more of myself, background, and journey was necessary in assuring families and the youth that my motivation was to utilize methods that would produce desired outcomes while allowing for strong connections to be built. The process of catalytic leadership involved building a relatable and dynamic process that engendered trust and empowered everyone along the way.

The third foundational characteristic, exemplary personal integrity, was critical to establish early in my role in the non-profit. The moment that leads to this transition from Athletic Director to the non-profit involved a deep reflection on my professional ethics. The reflection of that moment became a central point of consideration when working with individuals with both similar and dissimilar backgrounds to my own. The catalytic leader must understand how their personal integrity has been developed across cultural socialization processes. For example, if I am in a position of leadership where I am called on to lead others with similar ways of resolving conflicts, then it is incumbent upon me to maintain a calm disposition regardless of the intensity of the other person involved. This type of role integrity as a catalytic leader works across multiple environments. Whether I am in an educational system that is predominantly white, or leading a program situated in an urban area that is predominantly of color, my disposition becomes the catalyst for how conflict can be resolved.

Catalytic leadership is meant to be transformative and dynamic. Leading into the unknown will often require addressing complex challenges that are without precedent. When no precedents are present to guide leaders on how to make decisions in critical moments, catalytic leadership principles can be employed to steady the ship and guide organizations toward stable waters. I use *stable* instead of *safe* to illuminate the reality that safety is often illusory in tumultuous periods. Leading in the unknown will often prefer the steadying force, rather than the one seeking to make safe decisions. While safe decisions may maintain the status quo for a while, they often mask the underlying problems that exist. Catalytic leaders understand that even amid turbulent times, stabilizing the organization during difficult social realities is in itself a transformative kind of leadership. The catalytic leader is driven to ensure the most equitable outcomes across diverse groups while not transgressing core values and principles that act as guideposts to the process of leadership. I now turn to a profile of leadership of Dr. Tamica Smith-Jones to further demonstrate catalytic leadership principles.

PROFILE OF LEADERSHIP – DR. TAMICA SMITH-JONES

Dr. Tamica Smith-Jones is a study in perseverance and catalytic leadership. This profile in leadership is emblematic of the element of catalytic leadership that is gaining momentum over time. It is over time that Dr. Smith-Jones gained invaluable insight into aspects of leadership that has enabled her to vocationally advance. The foundational principles of catalytic leadership: 1) a continuous focus on desired results, 2) a sense of connectedness and relatedness, and 3) exemplary personal integrity, are all on ample display in Dr. Smith-Jones' professional journey. It is a privilege to present her story of catalytic leadership here.

Case Study: Dr. Tamica Smith Jones, Director of Athletics, University of California-Riverside/ Chief Operating Officer and SWA, Kennesaw State University

- Dr. Tamica Smith-Jones, Director of Athletics, University of California-Riverside
- 2008–13 (2008–9, interim) – Clark Atlanta University
- 2013–15 – Sr. Associate Athletic Director for Internal Affairs/SWA, University of Texas at San Antonio
- 2015–21 – Director of Athletics at UC Riverside
- 2021—Chief Operating Officer/SWA, Kennesaw State University

Defining Moment

The defining moment for me was getting the call from then President of Clark Atlanta University (CAU) to lead the Panthers program forward after leadership change (2008, Interim Athletic Director). I had worked for five years as a coach and senior woman administrator five years prior. I relieved myself of coaching duties a few years beforehand to find a bit more work life balance and to be of more administrative support to our athletics team. That decision was rewarding because I was able to spend more time with the coaches, student-athletes and staff, hear their concerns and escalate information to the athletics director more strategically. Once I transitioned into the interim role, I was already equipped with information relative to the strengths and opportunities within the program. With this information, I was able to unite the team, set strategic priorities, and move us forward seeking to win every day—and that we did—together!

The president said he would facilitate a national search, but after a successful year in the interim role he named me the permanent Athletics Director, a position I held for five successful years. A few successes included the first men's basketball championship in over 40 years, first winning football season, first volleyball championship—all with coaching hires I made during my tenure. Our academics soared from average 2.5 to above 3.0 cumulative grade point average across the 11 programs. Additionally, our student-athletes were ambassadors for the program and earning internships through intentional work I was doing to connect with the community and local businesses. Lastly, we re-established the Athletics Association and raised more than 100% more funding in support of our student-athlete success and capital projects.

Serving as the Athletics Director of Clark Atlanta University was one of the most rewarding periods of my career because I had a supportive president. The athletics program closely aligned with the mission of the university, utilized my vision and strong leadership, promoted team building skills to lead our team, and re-energized the campus community and fans around our student-athletes' success. In that season I realized I could do this—I could be a high performing Athletics Director and lead teams to great success!

Decision Making

A critical decision-making moment was my transition from Clark Atlanta University (CAU) Athletic Director to accepting a new role at UTSA as Sr. Associate Athletic Director for Internal Affairs/SWA. This moment was pivotal because I left my comfort zone and what was familiar. I took the opportunity for leadership in a city where I did not have a previous relationship. It was a true step of faith, but I wanted to strengthen my weaknesses and tap into athletic administrative opportunities I did not have at Division II Clark Atlanta University. For example, it was tough leaving a good situation at CAU, my president was supportive and saddened by the decision, saying he could not afford to keep me and wished me all the best. My family and friends did not understand why San Antonio, and why I could not find something local. While it cost me my comfort, it was one of the most pivotal moments in my role as a leader to step back into a #2 role. In hindsight, although I left CAU much better as a competitive program, I realized I did not do a good enough job preparing my successor in that transition. I have grown from this realization and now make it a part of all my leadership and transition planning.

Another decisive moment was transitioning from UTSA, Sr. Associate AD to accepting the offer as Director of Athletics at UC Riverside. Truly a pivotal moment as I had only been at UTSA for about 18 months before the opportunity was presented to me. Initially, I felt strongly that timing was not right as I was enjoying my role, learning, and making tremendous impact relative to diversity, equity, and inclusion work at UTSA. However, my supervisor was an internal influence and incredibly supportive of me at least looking at the opportunity. My supervisor revealed hating to lose me, but I can run my own department which helped me take the next step to interview. The external influence was Kevin Anderson, another minority athletics director who said when these opportunities come you must look because they do not come to us often. I know my decision would have a profound impact on those I was responsible for leading because I was the first African American in a senior athletics leadership position. I was aware this meant student-athletes would, for the first time, have that go-to person or representation. With that in mind I have been intentional in my leadership to ensure I have truly diverse recruitment and hiring practices so that with one person's transition it does not leave such a tremendous void.

Adding Value/Building Trust

I believe it is especially important to be familiar with who you are communicating with regardless of the reason for dialogue. For example, I get briefings and bios on donors and even prospective high-level recruited student-athletes who our coaches want me to meet and sell the vision of the program. As a minority leader I have heard references to us being labeled as aggressive rather than passionate. This misperception can threaten my ability to communicate to diverse audience. Another example is that I have heard reference to me being intense. With that, when people are familiar with you, I believe they can give you the grace as a leader we all need to communicate and not be censored to make people comfortable. Showing up fully and embracing our difference is critical in leadership.

Self-Care

I have maintained my faith by having a daily devotional time, meditating in the mornings, and working out on a consistent basis. In addition, I have purchased a new home workout machine to make sure I stay consistent. I am disciplined with my diet and what I allow in my spirit. I genuinely believe in keeping my mind, body, and spirit healthy, positive, and in alignment. I never want to be depleted in my mind, body, or spirit, because this is when I am prone to making mistakes, feeling negative, and not having a growth mindset.

PRINCIPLE TO PRACTICE

The catalytic leader demonstrates a dogged determination to make an impact in any organization. Dr. Tamica Smith-Jones provides a unique example of this determination through the acceptance of the leadership roles throughout her accomplished career. In just one year, she operated with such a palpable drive to achieve successful outcomes that she was rewarded with the full-time role. In her next two roles, she became attuned to the core attributes of catalytic leadership. Dr. Smith-Jones found success at forming partnerships across leadership structures, utilizing excellent communication skills to forge sustainable agreements, and developing expertise in the employment of diversity, equity, and inclusion principles. The latter enabled her to work seamlessly across multiple strategies, while sustaining tremendous momentum over time. Dr. Smith-Jones is truly a noteworthy catalytic leader.

Key Takeaways

- The catalytic leader is driven to ensure the most equitable outcomes across diverse groups while not transgressing core values and principles that act as guideposts to the process of leadership.
- Catalytic leaders are well versed in convening and joining with a diverse group of individuals, forging sustainable agreements, setting into motion multiple strategies, and sustaining momentum over time.
- Catalytic leaders focus on three foundational characteristics of strong leadership:
    1. A continuous focus on desired results
    2. A sense of connectedness and relatedness
    3. Exemplary personal integrity

CHAPTER FOUR

Building Trust in the Moment

Relational Bank Accounts: It's important to keep healthy relationship balances with those we lead. As the relationship matures, we make deposits and withdrawals in these imaginary accounts based on how we behave.

Based on excerpt from James C. Hunter, *The Servant: A Simple Story About the True Essence of Leadership*

FOUNDATIONAL WISDOM

Regardless of the predicament, trust in my ability to lead has always been the foundation that has sustained me personally, as a husband and father, mentor, and especially now as the Vice Chancellor and Director of Athletics at University of Missouri–Kansas City (UMKC). Deep introspection has led me to examine multiple elements of my career in this chapter. Like many administrators and executives, I experienced my share of disappointment, reluctance, and humility. The inherent difficulties of leading in the unknown often requires this reflection, along with an examination of cultural contexts, dimensional realities, and a determination whether current frameworks have the capacity to address new and unprecedented problems. As a result, dynamic responses are required for new and variable issues that arise in the unknown. Developing trust across organizations is essential when introducing new and dynamic frameworks during uncertain and unprecedented times.

Each time I have introduced a new framework it has required a measure of trust on the part of those I led. However, as leader it is imperative that we recognize the moment we require those we lead to make a deposit of trust, especially when they cannot be certain of the outcome–only certain that their leader has their best interest at heart. Fox, Davis, and Baucus (2020) posit that to lead in uncertain and unprecedented times, authentic leadership is a requisite to have a dynamic response and build trust for external and internal stakeholders. A list of authentic leadership, while not exhaustive, includes ethics, moral perspective, values, relational transparency, positive social interactions, self-regulation, consistency, and positive behavior modeling. I will explain these concepts of authentic leadership further in the principles of leadership section of this chapter.

Robert J. Wicks (2012) asked in his book *Riding the Dragon*, "Will we recognize and take this opportunity, or will we only focus on the suffering and miss the opportunities for radical inner change that this spiritual experience offers." Each time I make an investment as a leader it is evolutionary, whether it is the beginning of a new program, the recognition of an exceptional student-athlete, or acknowledging the over-and-above efforts of an often-overlooked employee. In that moment, I am planting a seed for what could be an institution level ground-breaking development, or the launching of a star athlete. However, each time I require those I lead to make a trust withdrawal on my behalf, it is an emotional experience as a leader. It is in this moment, I understand that I must raise my level of play. I must go to a place that I have never been before, and I must engender a new definition of excellence—demonstrate the ultimate form of leadership. In essence, it becomes a spiritual transformation.

MARTIN'S LEADERSHIP MOMENT

As a leader, the reality of the unknown sometimes taps you on the shoulder and demands that you make tough decisions. I have fought against the impossible for the majority of my life and I have had to make difficult decisions. However, the gravity of those decisions carries an entirely different weight when the result has the potential of impacting the lives and livelihoods of those who have placed an immeasurable amount of trust in you and what you do in your position as a leader. I am gravely in tune with the responsibilities inherent in leading in uncertain times. I recognize that the stakes for decision-making can cause a fissure in trust development that has multi-decade implications. The ripple effect of decision-making is a place of deep consideration in my current role.

Recounting the last two years which I have spent building my commitment to a "locked-in with locked arms" mentality as the incoming Athletics Director and now Vice Chancellor, I find myself revisiting the promises made to staff members and coaches as I am faced with furloughs, layoffs, position eliminations, and program suspensions. These individuals are some of the very same people who believed in the vision I offered for an attainable reality. Now I find myself faced with the tough decisions that will impact the athletic opportunities of over 70 student-athletes participating in two of our most successful Olympic sports.

It is difficult to ignore the range of emotions I feel in this moment. They make me the leader I am, but they also serve as a compass in this moment of the unknown. I am often deeply concerned with the potential ripple effect of decisions that will impact lives. I wrestle with the potential outcomes of decisions that will not only impact the relationship with me (the leader), but the institution as well. However, I have an obligation to do what is in the best interest of the university and campus community. I am increasingly cognizant of what is expected of me as I consider how to execute the university's mission and goals with only a fraction of my departmental staff members. Difficult, unprecedented, and uncertain times have caused me to recalibrate institutional priorities with augmented resources. The development of trust in this period has had to be adjusted as well. Trust is somewhat easier to build in the midst of a win or when experiencing an achievement. However, when facing the unknown, trust becomes a genuine test of authentic leadership.

PRINCIPLE OF LEADERSHIP

Dynamic flexibility is a familiar concept in the world of athletics. Over the years, strength and conditioning programs have increasingly recognized the importance of flexibility for peak performance (Hedrick, 2000). Professional athletes are extending careers well beyond what has been previously thought to be their "prime" due to a greater focus on pliability of musculature and maintenance of flexibility. I would like to borrow from the established wisdom of dynamic flexibility within the athletic world to speak about the need to infuse these principles into how we lead into the unknown. The importance of remaining flexible as a leader has never been more important regardless of indutsry or occupation.

High achievement in sports often involves a demanding and disciplined approach that requires maximum focus along with an ability to overcome adversity. In this way, leadership is not dissimilar. For athletes, the ability to have optimum flexibility provides a benefit for performance while minimizing risk of serious muscular injury. In the arena of play, as in life, variable conditions often introduce unforeseen challenges that will require the athlete to make real-time adjustments to their performance. If properly prepared, the athletes' range of motion increases to meet the challenges presented in their respective sport. In leadership, range of motion can be thought of as the broad portfolio of skills that allow for flexibility to handle myriad challenges that come with leading into the unknown. The individual skills in the portfolio can be analogized to the joints in the body, which each have a different threshold for flexibility. A leader, akin to an athlete, can have great flexibility in one area but a limited *range of motion* in another area. It is incumbent on leaders to develop dynamic flexibility to expand their capacity to overcome adversity in the unknown.

Dynamic flexibility training is thought to be more effective for athletes because it mimics the movements expected in the arena of play. Hedrick (2000) states, "Dynamic stretching consists of functional-based exercises that use sport-specific movements to prepare the body for activity." Leaders could learn much from this type of preparation. First, this type of training necessitates a working knowledge of the movements expected within a sport. Our best coaches spend an inordinate number of hours breaking down the movements within their respective sports to place athletes in the best position to win. Leaders who want to employ dynamic flexibility will study their industries to position their organization to win. An equally important lesson from dynamic stretching is that the body is prepared for specific skills germane to the sport. Leaders looking to have a flexible and dynamic organization will focus on growing the capacity to perform through persistent training that will increase the probability of dealing with adversity in uncertain times.

Shifting from athletics, much can also be learned about dynamic flexibility from the field of engineering. Dimitriadis and Pistikopoulos (1995) suggest that there are certain systems that must continue to operate during unprecedented and uncertain times. For example, plants that house chemicals or nuclear energy must maintain equilibrium, regardless of external conditions. In this context, flexibility is defined as "the ability to maintain feasible operation over a range of uncertain conditions" (Dimitriadis & Pistikopoulos, 1995). While the field of athletics is not in the category of chemical plants, it can have similar levels of toxicity that if not mitigated can threaten the maintenance of feasible operations. The presence of multiple stakeholders (e.g., coaches, student-athletes, university administrators, boosters, etc.) within the world of collegiate athletics necessitates a vigilant approach to leadership, particularly in *uncertain conditions*. Navigating all these constituent groups while upholding the best interest of the institution is the primary task of the dynamically flexible leader. I further submit that maintaining feasible operations over a range of uncertain conditions calls on leaders who are both flexible and authentic.

Authentic leadership qualities include ethics, moral perspective, values, relational transparency, positive social interactions, self-regulation, consistency, and positive behavior modeling (Fox, et.al., 2020). These authentic leadership qualities are not mutually exclusive. As a result, many will be intricately connected with one another. To begin, professional ethics are important as they set standards and expectations for behavior within organizations. When fear and anxiety are high in uncertain times, core ethics become steadying forces for organizations seeking to maintain equilibrium. Next, authentic leadership involves having and demonstrating a moral perspective consistent with the expressed mission of an institution. When crises arise, a critical question to be answered is how aligned the leader's morals with the mission of the institution are. In the public domain, confidence is often reassured during difficult crises when leaders emerge with the moral fortitude to assuage fears and doubts about an uncertain future.

Values are connected to moral perspectives within authentic leadership. Values are often a core set of concepts that undergird a leader's moral perspective. Values are the umbrella under which goals and objectives are developed within an organization. Adherence to values encourages the leader to act with consistent governance by demonstrating decision-making in times of crises. The next quality of relational transparency is often a result of an open explanation of how values were considered in the decision-making process. Relational transparency can be defined as the degree to which leaders are open about differentials in power based on both positional and cultural authority within organizations. Authentic leaders do not hide behind positional authority, where great distances are created between themselves and those within the organization. Authentic leaders realize that they set the tone for every supervisory relationship in the organization. It is critically important to promote equity in relationships across organizations for healthier interactions and increased productivity. When everyone feels like a part of the team, overall morale inevitably escaletes. This level of morale better prepares organizations in times of crisis and tumult.

Positive social interactions are an essential element of authentic leadership. The impact leaders have can be measured by how people feel post interaction. Do people feel empowered after an exchange with someone in leadership? Or do people feel deflated and demotivated to achieve the goals and objectives necessary for success? A focus on positive social interactions can help build a dynamic and flexible workforce capable of thriving in an uncertain future. Likewise, self-regulation is a quality of authentic leadership that is key for leading into the unknown. When a confluence of events collides to create unprecedented times, a tendency to match the chaotic energy is a trap for many leaders. Self-regulation takes on an entirely new level of importance for leaders seeking to bring calm to chaos. The steadiness created from a consistent self-regulation can provide an example for others as they try to figure out how not only to survive but thrive in the unknown.

Consistency, or the ability to maintain fidelity to principles of leadership, affords leaders the room to speak from a platform of confidence. The confidence is born of the knowledge that decisions are being made using the same set of core principles regardless of the external circumstances that may be occurring. While it is true that unprecedented events require an expanded capacity for dynamic and flexible decision-making, the authentic leadership qualities remain consistent. Closely aligned with consistency is positive behavior modeling, which, although self-explanatory, should not be underestimated in importance to leading in the unknown. In crises, the mind can tend to overly focus on negative inputs, which can lead to negative outputs. A solution for this is when authentic leaders model positive behavior that shifts the focus away from negativity. With this approach, a leader becomes a dynamic force that flexes an organization from a negative to positive orientation towards an unknown future. We will see many elements of authentic leadership in our next profile in leadership, Mark Ingram.

PROFILE OF LEADERSHIP – MARK INGRAM

Mark Ingram, Director of Athletics at the University of Alabama—Birmingham, is an example of an authentic leader who has had to display dynamic flexibility in his career. Unlike the average successful football player who dreamed of one day playing IN the National Football League (NFL), Mark had not yet contemplated his exit plan once he finished high school. In fact, it was not until a coach identified his talent during a football camp that he realized football could pave a path to college and later a career in athletics administration. Mark was able to pivot when he had a positive interaction with an effective leader. This interaction would have a profound impact on the values he would develop throughout his life.

Like most events in his life, Mark began the marketing process to sell his skill on the field by creating highlight tapes and applying to various colleges. As his senior year was ending, he began making calls to finalize his plan to attend the college of his choice only to find that there had been some major staff changes that pushed him out of the planned recruiting class. Devastated and unsure of his next move, Mark miraculously received a call from the coaching staff at the University of Tennessee with an offer he simply could not refuse. Recalling his first time on the Tennessee field in 1992, Ingram recalls the very moment he began building his value as a student-athlete, "I was locker number 124 with my name hand-written on a strip of medical tape. It all began with an internal progression." He spent three years as a walk-on accepting every opportunity presented to him as a chance to build personal value and equity as a teammate.

Confident in the value he brought to his team, Mark began his third year as a long snapper starter and was teammates with NFL legend Peyton Manning. Finishing his year with impressive stats and a Master's degree in Sports Administration, Mark began his administrative career with the University of Tennessee in 1998 as Assistant Director of Development. Therefore, similar to his days a standout student-athlete, Mark began his deliberate journey toward adding value.

Case Study: Mark Ingram, Associate Vice President and Director of Athletics, University of Alabama at Birmingham

- Mark Ingram, Associate Vice President/Director of Athletics at University of Alabama at Birmingham (2015-present)
- 1998–2002 Assistant Director of Development, University of Tennessee
- 2002–2005 Assistant Athletics Director for Development, University of Missouri
- 2005–2007 Assistant Athletics Director for Development, University of Georgia
- 2007-2012 Senior Associate Athletics Director for Development, University of Tennessee
- 2012–2015 Associate Vice President and Executive Senior Associate for Athletics, Temple University

Defining Moment

Building your value as a leader does not come in a moment, it occurs every time you lead, follow, listen, and react. From the moment I joined the Tennessee Volunteers Football Team as a walk-on center, I knew I needed them to not only see the value in my skill, but I had to build value in my dependency as player and my ability to go the extra mile as a teammate. So, from the moment I started practicing, I tried to make sure I was always on the roster for home games, and then I later pushed for the away game lineups. In every move I made, I wanted the coach to visually recall my contributions once I built up the courage to let him know that while I may not have been the smartest or biggest player, I was beyond doubt the best to be moved to the next level as a starter.

Decision Making

I was a member of the senior staff during a time that a new athletic director (AD) was hired. Though my unit had completed its best year in school history, the AD decided to eliminate my position. Was this because he wanted his own person, wanted to save money, wanted to restructure in some other way? Perhaps. I grieved like many would, I was sad, angry, depressed, confused, embarrassed… all those things. But, after just a few days to reconcile what happened, I was able to refocus and get to work finding the next opportunity. I met with several donors and several well-connected people who I thought could help me. What I learned is that you must help yourself… period. You must have the guts to tell people what has happened and that you are available. I started working my network and telling my story. One day a colleague called to tell me he had given my name to someone at another institution that had reached out looking for good candidates. He told me to look at it, and so I did. I interviewed, was offered the job, and accepted it. That was the best decision I ever made. Everyone in the industry told me not to take the job. They said I was not a good fit, and that the department was so small, I would **HAVE to do EVERYTHING**… and every time they said it, I always responded with the same thing. I said, "You do not understand. I do not have to do everything; **I GET to do** everything. That's why I'm taking the job." We must recognize as leaders that there is a lot of work getting done around us and that tasks no matter how big or small are opportunities to learn or grow and these are the things, we **GET to do**… not **HAVE to do.**

Adding Value/Building Trust

Our core values are simple by design. They are:

1. Win Championships
2. Graduate with Honors
3. Make a Difference

The intent is that all our staff and student-athletes can recite these any time they are asked. They are easy to remember and are simple enough to focus on with regularity. Spring sports were canceled mid-season, so we were not able to finish what we started but our men's golf team was having their best season ever, so we promoted that heavily to our fans so that they knew it was happening. Our student-athletes had their strongest academic semester in at least ten years. Finally, once the pandemic shelter was lifted and our student-athletes began returning to campus, one of the first things our football team did was a clean-up day around the community. In many ways, I think you build trust by following through on things that you talk about. You cannot just speak; you must back up what you say with action. That holds true today, just as it did prior to the pandemic.

Self-Care

Being at home has provided me a lot more flexibility with my schedule, so I have changed my routine for the better. I have gotten up earlier and have been able to exercise more than I have in a long time. I have maximized time on conference calls and coupled it with walks or other forms of exercise. I have done a lot of small household chores which I have found to be therapeutic and provided a lot of reflection time for work and family.

PRINCIPLE TO PRACTICE

Mark Ingram provides us with an excellent example of how trust invested in his early development paid dividends throughout his career. This portrait of an authentic leader who empowered Mark through a positive social interaction lends validity to the power of building trust in moments that change one's life trajectory. The trust placed in Mark led to the development of internal values and behavioral consistency which in turn set the foundation for demonstrating dynamic flexibility principles in both his athletic and vocational careers. In his athletic career, Mark positioned himself to succeed by focusing on a particular skill set that would increase his capacity to perform in the arena of play. He became dynamic in his skillset by preparing for all eventualities he would face on the field. The flexibility was shown as he transitioned from the practice squad to the starting lineup. When faced with challenges, Mark chose dynamic flexibility to express himself as an authentic leader in the locker room and on the field.

Lessons learned in athletics often parallel what is experienced in decisive moments of life. In these decisive moments, several factors determine successful outcomes. First, is the level of specific skill-based preparation that is a hallmark of dynamic flexibility. This preparation increases the capacity for leadership skillsets. The greater capacity builds trust across the organization that no matter the size of the problems, or uncertain the times, authentic leaders instill confidence that things will be properly handled. Next, the ability to maintain excellent functionality with diminished resources is a necessity for leaders at times. Dynamic flexibility promotes making real-time adjustments while not compromising core values and principles of an institution. Ultimately, dynamic flexibility principles and authentic leadership qualities have the ability to greatly enhance one's chances for successful outcomes.

Key Takeaways

- Leaders who adhere to dynamic flexibility principles seek to expand their capacity to overcome adversity in the unknown by expanding the *range of motion* in their skill portfolio.

- Leaders who adhere to dynamic flexibility principles demonstrate the ability to maintain feasible operations over a range of uncertain conditions.
- Dynamically flexible leaders operate with authentic leadership qualities to promote equity in relationships across organizations for positive interactions and increased productivity.

CHAPTER FIVE

Self-Reflection – Relevance in the Moment

> **"I believe that this is a moment with great potential for deep meaning."**
>
> Brandon E. Martin, "What to the Black Student-Athlete is the Fourth of July?"

FOUNDATIONAL WISDOM

The ability to define the parameters of winning or losing is not always as simple as a final score. Some wins have such a cost that the benefits are short lived and produce a string of losses on the backend. Some winning can impact characterological changes that are imperceptible at the beginning but emerge to shape thinking and behavior. For example, Idowu Koyenikan (2016) in *Wealth for All: Living a Life of Success at the Edge of Your Ability,* states "There will be times in your life that you will be challenged to choose between honor and something else... I am asking that you not sacrifice your honor for the sake of acquiring easy things." Winning often masks underlying issues that become hidden under the adulation and respect that accompany being a part of a successful program. The challenge is to develop processes of both internal and external reflection that have the ability to reveal who we are at the core.

Deep reflection often requires a level of vulnerability that has not always been engendered in my contextual environments. Most of my *Microsystem* (e.g., family of origin, neighborhood) and *Exosystem* (e.g., athletic programs, vocational environments) levels did not socialize me in ways that rewarded vulnerability. Growing up as an African American male in South Central Los Angeles, projecting strength and sublimating weaknesses was paramount to gain respect. Any sign of weakness was exploited and targeted which served to harden emotions into an impenetrable barrier. This outer shell became the persistent face to show to the world that nothing and no one could impact me. This shell would become a critical part of how I came to succeed in athletics. The term "alpha male" comes to mind when thinking about stepping on the basketball court and demanding respect. From this mentality, weakness was a liability to be conditioned out until at the very least, it became a strength. As I reflect, this type of hardened masculinity is the antithesis of vulnerability.

From this hardened position, the knowledge that I could fill a void through winning became my reality. In this reality, winning reinforced the need to not engage in deep reflection that opened places of vulnerability and brokenness. Akin to having the ball in my hand on the court, controlling the action, I learned to dictate the depth others could reach within me. In fact, I became adept at projecting strength while masking deeper vulnerabilities. I now recognize that hardened masculinity that does not allow for demonstrations of vulnerability is extremely unhealthy and can become potentially toxic for leading in the known and unknown. Confronting toxic masculinity is key to breakdown systems that reward strength and sanction weakness. Just like I learned in my neighborhood growing up, it affords you temporary respect while costing the ability to display a full range of emotions. These emotions become the cornerstones for how we communicate. Learning to be a mindful communicator first entails learning to be in touch with all parts of the self. Learning to communicate with all parts of oneself is critical for leading in the unknown.

MARTIN'S LEADERSHIP MOMENT

A main responsibility of my role as Vice Chancellor/Director of Athletics is to evaluate coaching candidates that will be a good fit for the development of student-athletes, maintaining program integrity, and building a winning culture. Across my athletic and administrative careers, I have been able to glean successful habits from phenomenally successful coaches and programs. Each coach and leader had distinctive characteristics that distinguished their style of leadership, but some common themes emerged that have come to inform my current approach to coaching selections. First, the successful coaches were able to maximize talents in their respective arena of play both from exceptional talents and those who were less talented but willing to work hard. Next, each leader had clearly defined principles that shaped program culture and climate which contributed to winning cultures. Another common area was discovered in the coaches' ability to effectively communicate expectations to student-athletes, other coaches, and athletic administrations. While this list is not exhaustive, it speaks to foundational areas I consider when hiring and evaluating coaches within the athletic program.

Most coaches who ascend to the upper echelon of coaching ranks have experienced many successes in their field. I am familiar with how the accolades of being associated with winning programs can inflate personalities who feel like their approach is unassailable. In addition to an emboldened personality, winning also produces an expected formula for success that leads to preferred modes of communication. This communication includes more than just methods, it considers the *who* involved, as much as the *what* being shared. The contextual environments in which leaders are socialized often produces who they become comfortable with in both giving and receiving instruction. I am well aware that as an African American athletic administrator, the line of familiar and comfortable communication between myself and coaches is a key point of consideration. I recognize that we are all products of our collective experiences, and coaches and athletic administrators are not immune from this fact. As a result, I often contend with exchanges where I am simultaneously navigating culture differences alongside presenting issues within the athletic program.

The hiring and evaluating process often comes with tense moments where cultural considerations are underlying factors in what is perceived by each party. For example, if I need to address a coach about one of three common factors outlined for successful programs: development of student-athletes, maintenance of program integrity, or building a winning culture, I have to navigate through several factors in order to achieve a desirable outcome. One key factor is the level of cultural comfort between administrator and coach. If each of us has been forged in environments that equate fear of rejection or loss as weakness, then we will both present as uncompromising when trying to work through a model for program success. In addition, if we happen to come from different cultural backgrounds (i.e., race, ethnicity, socio-economic status), then it may be the first time a coach has had to receive instruction from a cultural other. Specifically, in my case it may be the first time a coach has had to receive instruction from an African American administrator. These dynamics often go underexamined within the realm of leadership. Leading into the unknown will require an ability for deep cultural reflection and mindful leadership that addresses how we deal with ourselves while collaborating with others.

PRINCIPLE OF LEADERSHIP

Mindful leadership encapsulates the ability for deep cultural reflection and effective communication (Ehrlich, 2017). Within mindful leadership is a deep understanding that on some level, we each need to be validated to establish self-worth. As with most words, multiple definitions are available that provide slightly different meanings. For example, a formal definition of validation is to make valid; substantiate; confirm. While technically correct, it does not capture the complexity of working in a culturally rich environment where one is called to the task of understanding multiple layers of identity. Further, this definition does not reflect a sense of responsibility placed on the leader to come prepared to validate a salient identity that may be important to an employee in a cultural exchange. A more culturally relevant definition of validation is providing truth to one's own cultural story. Cultural perspective is a key to understanding what people need to be validated when during either a cultural or organizational exchange. Mindful leadership offers several components to consider achieving successful outcomes that acknowledge the truth of one's own cultural story.

According to Ehrlich (2017), research on mindful leadership has been recently associated with benefits to: "(1) focus, decision-making, memory, creativity, and learning; (2) communication, collaboration, and productivity; (3) emotional intelligence, well-being, and internal and client relationships; (4) job satisfaction and engagement; and (5) reduced stress, absenteeism, and turnover." These benefits, when combined with a cultural lens, have a great capacity to increase a leader's ability to lead among diverse audiences and environments. Mindful leadership has six distinguishing characteristics: spirit, emotion, mind, body, connecting, and inspiring. Each of these will be explored, with the added cultural implications for a culturally informed, mindful leadership. In the figure below, you will find the interrelated nature of mindful leadership and how each component produces outcomes with the potential for sustainable success.

The spirit component does not have overtly religious or faith-based connotations, but it certainly can contain elements of various understandings of ecclesial practices. In the framework of mindful leadership, spirit has four factors that should motivate leaders. First is a deep desire to a greater good recognized as a calling or purpose. This factor deeply resonates with me as I lean heavily into being guided by a greater purpose to make a generational impact. Next, is an adherence to core values that become cornerstones for ethical and moral decisions. In my experience as an administrator, I have found that solving surface conflicts often comes with sorting out underlying value differences. The third spirit characteristic is understanding that you are connected to something beyond yourself. This fits well within my personal definition of impact, in that individual efforts should always be tied to the outcomes for others. The last aspect of spirit involves being willing to deeply experience a full range of emotions. A willingness to be vulnerable enough to fully feel love, grief, or appreciation opens the door to greater alignment, connection, and communication between leaders and staff. Spirit is an essential component to mindful leadership that expands a leader's capacity to have a sustainable purpose with generative outcomes that have long-term impact.

The emotion component is strongly associated with spirit. In particular, the call to vulnerability within spirt that focuses on a deep reflection of our emotional selves. In recent years, much has been made of emotional intelligence. That is, the ability to know what you feel and ultimately use the data in between to reach successful outcomes. The cultural complexity of this exchange is worth exploring here. As an African American administrator, I am aware of certain stereotypes associated with emotional expressions from people who look like me. The trope of "Angry Black Man" (ABM) is a typical expression for when passion is displayed in an intercultural exchange. For example, if I am in a meeting with someone from European descent, they may come predisposed to believe in the ABM stereotype which will skew what is actually happening in the meeting. This potential misunderstanding may unduly impact the read of emotions which in turn creates negative reactions such as fear and distrust. As a culturally informed mindful leader, it is important to understand how emotions can be influenced by cultural factors and the stereotypes. Understanding the emotion component can lead to more positive interactions that impact mutual motivations to produce successful outcomes.

The mind component is about managing the incessant distractions that prevent clarity of thought and conscious. So often, leaders are distracted by the daily fires that consume much of their mental space. In recent times, the confluence of the pandemic, social uprisings due to continued racial injustice, and the economic downturn have created so many unprecedented challenges that finding space for critical thinking is a rare and precious commodity. Erhlich (2017) offers a framework for how to enter into a period of intentional silence to quiet the mind and reach a place of mental clarity: "1) Backward: What happened yesterday, and can I do better? 2) Forward: Where am I going in my business and career? 3) Inward: Am I staying true to my values and purpose? 4) Outward: What impact am I having on others and on my objectives?" I would add a fifth question to this framework to address cultural impact. Following the same framework, my question is: Onward: have I attended to the diversity within myself and others? The *mind* in mindful leadership is what allows for thoughtful decision-making in critical moments.

The body component in mindful leadership is important as many links have been made between physical, emotional, and cognitive fitness. As a former athlete, I understand the confidence of knowing my body was in peak condition and its impact on my performance. While my prime athletic years are past, I am still attentive to the body/mind connection in its ability to produce positive results. For example, healthy diet, sleep, and exercise regiments are largely recognized as factors to increase our immune systems and general sense of alertness. Another aspect to the body component is body language, which is a powerful communicator in cultural interactions. Verbal communication, while powerful, is only partly explanatory of what we takeaway post exchanges with others. We must come to understand that body language greatly influences how we respond to both the message and the person communicating. I am constantly aware of my body language in situations due to my general awareness of how people may be more interested in interpreting my *body* (i.e., skin color), than the *language* being communicated. The body component has the capacity to shift dynamics for the individual leader, as well as everyone they are coming into contact within the organization.

The previous four components of the mindful leadership model (spirit, emotion, mind, and body) are framed as what is necessary to *being present*. A mindful leader understands that their presence has the capacity to shift the atmosphere in each moment, or for the entirety of an organization. The last two components of the model are *connecting* and *inspiring*. Connecting is the ability to fully embrace and validate the lived experience of others. The successful leader can connect only when they are open to understand the cultural experience of others, especially when it is dissimilar from their own lived experiences. When a gap exists between understanding the cultural realities of the other, connection is threatened and processes towards successful outcomes may be severely disrupted. It is the responsibility of a leader to close the connection gap to make possible the ability to inspire. Inspiration can be thought of as breathing life into or awakening the full creative potential of a person.

I contend it is difficult to inspire without connecting first. Further, it is difficult to connect if one is not fully present with others. In this way, mindful leadership requires leaders to establish daily practices of reflection that can gauge the level of presence, connection, and inspiration. We will now turn to a profile in leadership, Jill Bodensteiner, who has embodied mindful leadership principles across her career.

PROFILE OF LEADERSHIP – JILL BODENSTEINER

Jill Bodensteiner continues to forge a distinguished career where she demonstrates the various aspects of mindful leadership. In this profile of leadership, you will see elements of validation, communication, and being present in critical moments that are emblematic of mindful leadership. In addition, you will clearly see the points of connection and inspiration that make Jill Bodensteiner a leader well positioned to lead into the unknown.

Case Study: Jill Bodensteiner, Director of Athletics, Saint Joseph's University

- Jill Bodensteiner, Director of Athletics, Saint Joseph's University
- 1997–2009 Associate Vice President & Senior Counsel, University of Notre Dame
- 2009–13 Associate Athletics Director, University of Notre Dame
- 2013–18 Senior Associate Athletics Director, University of Notre Dame
- 2018–Present Director of Athletics, Saint Joseph's University

Defining Moment

The unprecedented nature of the pandemic and the uncertainty it produced at the beginning, shifted many dynamics from a leadership perspective. As a leader, excellence in this season is also about how you share and express empathy. I can recall a moment on March 13, 2020 driving home and calling each one of my head coaches. Listening to their concerns, fears, and thoughts on moving forward was critical. Hearing the care that they had for the student-athletes and their safety was assuring. It was a series of multiple moments of empathy, trust, and bonding.

Decision Making

I have come to understand a major component of decision-making in leadership is being a good partner with the university. This involves making a commitment to communication. We are in a time when leaders must accelerate the ways in which they communicate. Having a deeper understanding of who, where, when, and how is critically important when communicating in this unprecedented period where things are changing rapidly. In keeping with the rapid pace of current times, I am cognizant about how we "tell our story" in this period. We have diversified our messaging by incorporating videos, maximizing our social media platforms, periodic messages to fans from student-athletes, and strategic communications from our coaches.

I am a lot more collaborative and patient. I process information very quickly and, in the past, I have not been the most patient regarding getting to the solution of a problem. I have been forced to slow down and be much more deliberate, self-aware, and empathetic. In short, I have become a more mindful leader.

Adding Value/Building Trust

During these unprecedented times, my core values have been strengthened. Integrity, resilience, innovation, excellence, diversity, and inclusion are deeply woven in everything we do in our department, particularly as it relates to student-athlete welfare and development. I have used this time to reflect on how I can further ingrain our core values into the ethos of our athletics department. This goes back to my point about communication. In this time when we are forced to be more fluid than normal, it is important to remind our coaches, staff, and student-athletes about what we stand for and the values that will make us persevere moving forward.

Self-Care

While I am aware of the need to maintain a healthy diet and exercise regularly, I have placed an emphasis on my mental health. I make sure to mentally prepare and get equipped for the challenges ahead. I understand the importance of having a renewed mind each day to handle the unprecedented challenges that continue to manifest themselves. While the pandemic has rightly placed a focus on physical well-being, our collective mental health should not be neglected. I am for anyone taking the time to attend to mental health and emotional well-being.

PRINCIPLE TO PRACTICE

Key Takeaways

- Mindful leaders seek to validate others through a cultural lens that honors their diverse lived experiences (e.g. backgrounds, perspectives, cultural truths).
- Mindful leaders will ask the following questions for daily clarity:

- **Backward**: What happened yesterday and can I do better?
- **Forward**: Where am I going in my business and career?
- **Inward**: Am I staying true to my values and purpose?
- **Outward**: What impact am I having on others and on my objectives?
- **Onward**: Have I attended to the diversity within myself and others?

  (Ehlrich, 2017)

- Mindful leaders have a willingness to be vulnerable enough to fully feel love, grief, or appreciation that opens the door to greater alignment, connection, and communication between themselves and staff.

CHAPTER SIX

Social Justice – Empowered in Every Moment

> "We live in a system that espouses merit, equality, and a level playing field, but exalts those with wealth, power, and celebrity, however gained."
>
> Derrick Bell, *Ethical Ambition: Living a Life of Meaning and Worth*

FOUNDATIONAL WISDOM

A perceptual distance often exists between rhetoric and reality. Rhetoric is a verbal strategy that is used to persuade or deter people into thinking that something is or is not actually occuring. Reality presents as a harsh reminder that no amount of rhetoric can mask injustices visited upon people on a daily basis. The rhetoric of an *even playing field* is often used to describe collegiate athletics, though the disparities between conferences, institutions, and experiences of student-athletes is far too palpable to ignore. No greater example of the actual gap between the *even playing field* rhetoric and actual experience of social injustice exists than the plight of Black student-athletes in major college athletics. The critical question becomes, what does social justice look like for those student-athletes who are celebrated for their athletic talents and gifts, but not fully embraced or respected outside of their uniforms?

The inquiry into social justice begets more questions. Are our institutions currently oriented towards understanding the world of our Black student-athletes? Are strategic priorities in athletic departments and collegiate institutions aligned with social justice principles that honor both the *student* as well as the *athlete*? Are mechanisms in place to ensure equitable access to academic and social resources that ensure a well-rounded experience? Are athletes interacting with culturally competent coaches and administrators during times of social unrest and societal change? Are institutions committed to ensuring the completion of academic goals and professional development in the event of an abrupt end to an athletic collegiate career? Are there readily accessible mechanisms to report mental or physical distress outside of specific coaching structures? Are athletic leadership structures aware of and committed to implementing best practices in diversity, equity, and inclusion approaches to leading programs? While this list is not exhaustive, it may be a good starting place to examine baselines for current practices in any college athletic organization.

MARTIN'S LEADERSHIP MOMENT

I have often spoken about my time while a basketball student-athlete at USC. While I have fond memories of that period, I contemplate the gap between the rhetoric I was given and the reality of my experience. For example, my deep love of the game of basketball often carried me through the persistent demands of practices, games, and academic demands. I was not given a blueprint on how to successfully navigate my collegiate experience, which at times was overwhelming. The mental and physical taxation was only partially mitigated by some of the perks of collegiate athletics. As a young man, free gear and apparel was appealing given that I had to purchase these items prior to receiving my collegiate scholarship. Another temporary salve was attention received from adoring fans. I stress the temporary nature of these perks, because they masked the intensity felt daily. I was aware enough to know that my profile afforded me a platform that, again, little guidance was provided on how to maximize. Fortuitous interventions by mentors gave me exposure to athletic administration on the back end of my collegiate career which would become a template for the rest of my career. Without this exposure, I could have become singularly focused on professional athletics without rounding out the rest of my academic talents and abilities. I have come to recognize that what often lies beneath experiences of Black student-athletes is a hyper-focused effort on the scoreboard while suffering in silence. From this experience of being a Black student-athlete at a predominantly white institution, I have embraced three "Rs" in my journey towards social justice: relatable, respectable, and relational.

As with many Black student-athletes, sports were a pathway for me to attend one of the finest institutions in the world, the University of Southern California (USC). Growing up in the shadow of USC in South Central Los Angeles, finding models that were authentically oriented towards successful outcomes was difficult. Fortunately, my hard-working father provided an example for me that was *relatable*. I now work in higher education among some of the best minds in the world. However, at heart I am the son of a blue-collar father who sacrificed to give me the opportunity to succeed. This foundation guides my consciousness for how I seek to be a relatable presence for others. This is especially true for Black student-athletes. I understand what it is like to have a continual test of acceptance, as I am still aware that both my stature and skin color will be threatening to some, despite my degrees and career accomplishments. I have observed the same perspectives taken towards Black student-athletes. While in their respective jerseys and on the field of play they are cheered, but "beyond the logo" they are misunderstood. I have always sought to be an authentic presence that is *relatable* and *reachable* as Black student-athletes endure their test of acceptance.

Two aspects of respect are deeply important to me: self-respect, and respect of others. The circle of Black men who raised me, including my father, taught that respect is the single most important factor in life. The lessons I remember most are what happens when you lose respect from peers, significant others, and community. I was taught about the consequences of being disregarded in one's own home, in the workplace, and in society. The resultant devastation of losing respect that was described to me was enough to light an eternal fire in my soul to command respect and offer respect to those with similar stakes. As a young man, I thought the rewards of accomplishment and respect were the common trappings of money, cars, and fine homes. As I have matured, I have come to realize that respect is not solely equated with these tangible symbols. The fire that still burns for respect is now focused on having the daily respect of my spouse and children. I want to be an example of a servant leader for my community, student-athletes, and those who society seeks to dishonor due to rampant injustices. I want to live a life of respect that shows them that getting knocked down is temporary, but the respect you earn in a comeback is permanent.

Robert K. Greenleaf, the progenitor of servant leadership, argues, "The servant-leader is servant first, it begins with a natural feeling that one wants to serve, to serve first, as opposed to, wanting power, influence, fame, or wealth" (Greenleaf & Spears, 2002). This framework of leadership as a servant first resonates with me for several reasons. First, I recognize that power, influence, fame, or wealth will not take away the social injustices experienced as a Black man. As mentioned earlier, I have been fortunate to be a collegiate and professional athlete, and administrator in major athletic programs. None of these accomplishments have mitigated the daily slights that accompany being a Black athletic administrator or student-athlete. As a result, I am focused on my assignment as a servant-leader to build relationships that produce outcomes beyond winning and losing. I want my relational presence to build solid character and academic excellence that develops well-rounded individuals who will have opportunities beyond the domain of play. I am committed to establishing relationships through service, because at the end of the day my work is not about self-fulfillment. My work, presence, and legacy will be built on how I served others.

PRINCIPLE OF LEADERSHIP

Social injustices like racism, discrimination in housing and employment, disparities in education, lack of access to health care, and the prevalence of police brutality continue to be a toxic fly in our societal ointment. Any one of these injustices alone is extremely injurious and can negatively impact how one lives. The simple fact is that for many, these injustices rarely show up in the singular. The plurality of injustices that people of color deal with daily presents as compounding experiences that cause disparities and gaps across societal structures. The additive stress of injustices is particularly acute for Black student-athletes across intercollegiate athletics. The stark gap between playing a sport in our cathedrals of athletics (e.g., arenas and fields) and then sitting in classes with students from backgrounds that would rarely, if ever, have occasioned crossing paths is a stunning reality. Any equity experienced on the court or field is quickly erased in the classroom and off campus. This is a challenge of social injustice facing every athletic program, from which no one is exempt. To think a program can be run without addressing social justice is like thinking one can jump in water and not get wet. We have a moral imperative to address social justice and create culturally safe environments for student-athletes.

Cultural safety is a concept that originated in the field of nursing to address systemic injustices in healthcare disparities (Browne et al., 2009). I contend that the core principles of cultural safety can be applied to the field of intercollegiate athletics to address social injustices. The primary foci of cultural safety are addressing power imbalances and inequitable social relationships with particular attention given to racial injustice. Cultural safety also acknowledges and validates the structural inequities and deleterious social conditions resultant from historical political and economic decisions from systemic oppression of people of color. Additionally, a core goal of cultural safety is disrupting typical race-based conversations that seek to minimize the importance of racial injustices.

This minimization of racial injustice is particularly harmful for Black student-athletes seeking to build confidence and prepare for a world that often rejects many aspects of who they are away from the arena of play.

An adapted definition of cultural safety for the world of intercollegiate athletics is curating intentional practices that counter tendencies in athletic programs which create cultural risk (or unsafe) situations that arise when minoritized people are degraded, reduced, or disempowered by the actions of majoritized people in power. This definition will require leaders of programs to embrace a social justice curriculum that frames four key foundations for cultural safety and change. Each foundation will require leaders proficient in cultural knowledge translation, which is the ability to have deep knowledge of the experience and realities of cultural others' journey of injustice.

The first foundation for cultural knowledge translation is understanding the history of lived experience told from the perspective of the oppressed, not the perspective of the oppressor. This foundation requires as much unlearning of unjust narratives of domination learned in our systems of education, as listening, and learning directly from communities of color. The next foundation is having clearly articulated goals that promote social justice and equity which are linked with an expanded notion of successful program outcomes. In this way, winning without equitable outcomes for student-athletes of color in academic and life preparation should not be seen as successful outcomes. The third foundation is creating structures of accountability where leaders are consistently engaged with determining the efficacy of social justice interventions. These accountability structures should aim to increase and maintain a critical consciousness of social justice that reinforces all decision making should be seen through a social justice lens. The last foundation is having social justice-oriented leaders select content that opens spaces for open dialogue that honors and validates organizational structures and inequities that are producing injustices for minoritized people in athletic programs. These foundations can provide a framework for leadership structures seeking to create cultural safety. Our profile in leadership, Patti Phillips, has spent her career seeking to create spaces that disrupt and challenge social inequities.

PROFILE OF LEADERSHIP – PATTI PHILLIPS

Patti Phillips has spent her career disrupting the narrative of limitation for women in sports. Advancing social justice issues for women in sports has been a demonstrated passion evidenced by the many women she has coached and mentored in various roles in the sports landscape. In this profile of leadership, you will view Patti's passion to make sincere change and be a positive force for women in sports. Patti Phillips is truly a champion of social justice and an exemplar for leaders who seek to make a substantial difference in their respective spheres of influence.

Case Study: Patti Phillips, Chief Executive Officer, Women Leaders in College Sports

- Patti Phillips, Chief Executive Officer, Women Leaders in College Sports
- 1997–99 Life Skills Program Coordinator, NCAA
- 1999–2010 Executive Director, WIN for KC (Women Intersport Network for Kansas City)
- 2010–Present Chief Executive Officer, Women Leaders in College Sports

Defining Moment

Creating connection points in times of social isolation is critical to breakdown the silence that often accompanies social inequities and injustices. I have started a "COVID-19 Circle" that is all about resources, ideas, testimonials, and community. This has aided in connectivity, trust, and growth mindset among staff and membership. I have been intentional about "doubling down" on our core values of excellence, leadership, diversity, equity, education, advocacy, empowerment, and commitment. This period has forced us to go deeper with our values and have them demonstrated in our decision-making and strategic planning. I am much more accessible to staff. I do not travel nearly as much so my calendar is open to focus more on our team. I have strongly encouraged my staff to spend as much time with their families as possible.

Decision Making

Social justice-oriented thinking is about having the ability to execute in our mission towards greater equity and inclusion in sports. The plain reality is that this is a time where we all must pay the bills, and leaders should be doing everything in their power to ensure that environments we create enable everyone to do that. Excellence in this season is all about staying true to purpose, drawing synergies with like organizations and groups, and making sure people are growing in these challenging times. There is no doubt that it is a difficult time, but also a time of great opportunity and advancement. I feel better now than

I did before 2020. Those who have been working on social justice have been present and those who have not are late to the table. It is more reactionary than authentic. I believe this is a time to be self-reflective and to figure out how each one of us can be the change we want to see in the world.

Adding Value/Building Trust

Our work is naturally challenging and when mindful of social justice can deplete our natural resources under the best circumstances. With the confluence of the pandemic, uprise of awareness with racial injustice, and downturn of the economy, I have seen our collective energy wane under the constant stress. As a result, I have been mindful of bringing even more energy than normal to meetings, Zoom calls, and presentations. I am a high energy person by nature, but I bring even more now. I am collaborative, direct, optimistic, and transparent. This has allowed me to build trust in a time when folks are concerned about feeding their families and paying their bills.

Self-Care

I am really disciplined in this area. I prioritize hydration, using food as fuel, exercise regularly, and focus heavily on breath work. I truly believe being in tune with my breathing is critical to maintain an open mind and clear thoughts. I am also big on daily affirmations and positive self-talk.

PRINCIPLE TO PRACTICE

Patti Phillips is certainly a leader with the capacity to lead in these unknown and uncertain times. A paragon of social justice leadership, Patti has dedicated her life to the uplift of women in sports. Inspirational in nature, she has used sports as a vehicle for female empowerment to disrupt the notions of what limits can be placed on girls and young women. Patti demonstrates how creating spaces to discuss difficult things engenders cultural safety in environments under her leadership. In keeping with my definition of cultural safety for the world of intercollegiate athletics, she is curating intentional practices that counter tendencies in athletic programs that create cultural risk (or unsafe) situations. I honestly believe that Patti's work with women is a template for how leaders can actively fight for minoritized people who are being degraded, reduced, or disempowered by the actions of majoritized people in power.

Key Takeaways

- Leaders seeking to create cultural safety will curate intentional practices that counter tendencies in athletic programs to create cultural risk (or unsafe) situations that arise when minoritized people are degraded, reduced, or disempowered by the actions of majoritized people in power.
- Leaders seeking to create cultural safety will identify and implement a social justice curriculum that leaders across the entire organization.
- Leaders understand that cultural safe environments actively challenge structural inequities that reinforce social injustices that negatively impact people and communities of color.

CHAPTER SEVEN

Profiles in Leadership – Timeless Wisdom for All Moments

"The ultimate measure of a man is not where he stands in moments of comfort and convenience, but where he stands at times of challenge and controversy."

Martin Luther King, Jr.,
"Strength to Love" (1963

INTRODUCTION

It is not an understatement to say that since March of 2020 we have been in unprecedented times with the onset of the global COVID-19 pandemic, early stages of societal unrest sparked by police brutality, and the resultant economic downturn that disrupted millions of lives. Intercollegiate athletics was not immune from these events, and perhaps as a reflection of society, has experienced upheaval to normal processes like never before. In these moments, we all seek ways forward through uncertainty that help to stabilize our lives. Further, we all are seeking any signs that signal an end to the additive stress on our careers, families, and communities. This chapter engages with several leaders who have lived and adjusted how they have navigated through these unprecedented times. As mentioned in the introduction, I will begin with expanded interviews that matched the shifting and often intensified realties as time progressed with the pandemic and continued fight for social justice. In the first two profiles, you will find leaders referencing pivotal moments in their previous experience that laid the groundwork for their current leadership. It is an honor to present these thought leaders who will offer timeless wisdom born of the many struggles of this moment.

Featured Leadership – Leading in the Unknown 2020

Allen Greene, Director of Athletics
Auburn University

As you contemplate your career, how would you define that critical moment when you realized you could make an impact in college athletics?

> When I was a fundraiser at Ole Miss, a donor who I had been cultivating made a six-figure commitment toward a very important capital project. It was during the phone call that I realized my relationships with donors had an actual impact on the student-athlete experience.

Thinking of at least three pivotal moments throughout your role as a leader, describe decisions you made in those moments that had a profound impact on those you were responsible for leading.

> Within the first few months as the AD at Buffalo, we made the decision to discontinue 4 sports. The decision was necessary based on the department/ university financial position. In this particular instance we only sought feedback from university leadership, but considered the impact that the decision would

have on student-athletes, coaches, staff, alums and donors.

This might be an unconventional response, but accepting the AD job at Auburn was definitely a pivotal moment. As the first Black AD to lead Auburn Athletics, and one without previous ties to the university, history was made with my hire. Simply put, my wife and I made the decision because institutional values aligned with our family values. We knew that the industry would take notice and provide encouragement for minorities who aspired to be an AD.

As the AD at Auburn, publicly addressing race in America was difficult personally and professionally. I had conversations with coaches and with University leadership prior to taking a public stance. I was uncertain about the public reaction, and was relieved that the responses were overwhelmingly positive.

Reflecting on your career in leadership, what is your preferred communication style? What recent adjustments have you made when communicating person-to-person verses virtually or utilizing a device and/or the media?

My personal communication style is definitely face-to-face. The pandemic has made it difficult, if not impossible to do so. Previously, I would have rarely used something like FaceTime to communicate, but now we find that video conferences like Zoom are widely accepted and I use it regularly. Though it doesn't replace human interaction, I can at least see body language of those on the call.

Describe the importance of timing when communicating to those you are leading.

If by "timing" you mean making sure that the recipient is in the right "headspace" to receive the information then I think it's about knowing your colleagues and doing the best you can to ensure successful communication.

As a leader, you have acquired a variety of professional experiences that has added value to your institutions, programs, and organizations. In recent months, how have you added value to the following:

    a. Family

    b. Athletics Department/University

    c. Supervisors and Stakeholders (i.e. Chancellor/ President, Board of Trustees, Donors)

Not sure if I have added value to my family. Though I'm home more, I'm actually busier than "normal." One benefit though is I'm always on time for dinner. For both b and c, I'm a transparent and authentic person by nature and the feedback that I've received is that our constituents are pleased by those character traits.

As a leader, what measures do you take or have taken to keep your staff/coaches focused and engaged on the departmental mission and core values?

I reiterate our guiding principles when engaged in discussions to keep our focus, and challenge everyone to hold me accountable to those principles as well during the decision-making process. The best way I know how to gain/maintain trust is to be transparent, even if the news is bad. While I'm optimistic, I have to be realistic as well. Again, we do Zoom calls to share information with coaches/staff as much as we can handle and I let them know that there is no question off limits. It's a crazy time and don't assume that we've already thought of a question.

Leadership roles in college athletics are often demanding and stressful. Describe activities you have incorporated to maintain self-care. Routines? ? ? Personal Time Away? ? ? Physical Activities?

I'm great at giving sound advice, but terrible at following it myself. I try to exercise several days a week, and find that working out keeps me alert during the day and helps me sleep better at night. Golf is therapeutic for me as well, so fresh air every couple of weeks serves as stress reducer.

Loss and defeat are just as much a part of leadership as winning and overcoming. Like cheering and celebration come with the wins, so do tears and grief with loss. In general, how do you process grief? ? ? How do you process loss? ? ? Describe a defining moment in your career where one or both were a necessary part of your journey as a leader.

As leaders, we shouldn't get too high or low, and that is one piece of advice I've been able to apply. I've learned to embrace the journey and be thankful for the good days and prepare for the bad ones.

As the Deputy AD at Buffalo, we made a coaching change in men's basketball. Many couldn't understand why, or didn't believe the new coach would be successful. Two years later, we won our first ever conference championship, and secured an automatic bid to the NCAA Tournament for the first time in school history. As the clock hit zero, I hugged some staff who were around and simply said, "we did it." I was so happy for those who had worked in the department for such a long period of time and finally got to be part of history. What a great feeling, and I think we partied that night like it was 1999.

Featured Leadership – Leading in the Unknown 2020

Chris Reynolds, Vice President for Intercollegiate Athletics, Bradley University

As you contemplate your career, how would you define that critical moment when you realized you could make an impact in college athletics?

At the start of my second year in law school (1994), I determined that I wanted to work on a college campus with the goal of mentoring young people. It was not my goal specifically to work in an athletics department. I simply wanted to have access to college aged students and working on a college campus in any capacity, in any unit on college campus, would provide me an opportunity to positively influence the lives of young people.

During the summer of 1994, I visited the NCAA national office, located in Overland Park, Kansas. After spending the day at the office, meeting a variety of staff people and asking them about their career experiences, I began to think that a career in athletics administration could potentially land me on a college campus, which became my ultimate goal.

Thinking of at least three pivotal moments throughout your role as a leader, describe decisions you made in that moment that had a profound impact on those you were responsible for leading.

As a leader in college athletics, I never really know the extent to which I am or have impacted the lives of student-athletes. It is my sense that my mere presence and the way in which I care for our student-athletes has an impact on them based upon comments I receive from graduating seniors. I'm finding it is the little things I do that matter most. The conversations I have with student-athletes to encourage them academically, athletically, and emotionally during challenging moments in their lives have made profound impacts in ways I did not consider at the time. I have found that people don't care how much you know, until they know how much you care. Taking time for people to get to know and hear them is important.

Outside of college athletics, my wife, Katrina, and I have mentored scores of college aged students who have not participated in athletics. We do our best to keep in touch with them. These students live in various parts of the United States of America and the world and have become an important part of our family. Katrina and I never limited our impact on college aged students to those who participated in athletics. We find that students on campus actually have more of a need for emotional support since they do not have teammates or a mature peer group to care for them.

Reflecting on your career in leadership, what is your preferred communication style? What recent adjustments have you made when communicating person-to-person verses virtually or utilizing a device and/or the media?

I would describe myself as an assertive communicator which means that I am adept at communicating my own feelings and ideas while considering the needs of others. I spend more time listening when communicating virtually. It's important that my team knows that I am interested in what they have to say and I want to know what is on their minds. I cannot learn what is on their minds if I am dominating the discussions.

Describe the importance of timing when communicating to those you are leading.

Timing is everything. I must sense when our staff and coaches need to hear from me. During a pandemic, it's important for staff, coaches, and student-athletes to know that I want to engage them in conversation. Consequently, as the leader, it is important that there is regular and ongoing communication occurring within and among the various areas of the department so that everyone is in the information loop. Moreover, everyone in the department must know that they have direct access to me or someone in the department who can field any of their questions.

As a leader, you have acquired a variety of professional experiences that has added value to your institutions, programs, and organizations. In recent months, how have you added value to the following:

a. Family

b. Athletics Department/University

c. Supervisors and Stakeholders (i.e. Chancellor/ President, Board of Trustees, Donors)

I have added value to my family by being present at home more. As a family, we have experienced wonderful conversations over the past three months and have grown closer.

The most important thing I can do for our staff and coaches is to express my care and concern from them and their families. Every decision made during this challenging time must be made with them in mind. During challenging times, empathy is important to model and treating everyone with dignity and respect is essential.

At the beginning of the pandemic in our country, our university announced the hiring of a new president. Helping our new president get acclimated to and knowledgeable of our current campus culture has brought value to him and consequently, to our university.

As a leader, what measures do you take or have taken to keep your staff/coaches focused and engaged on the departmental mission and core values?

My aim is always to live out our department's core values. Staff and coaches must see me exemplify on a daily basis the ideals I expect all others to demonstrate. Since most of my communication with staff and coaches is limited to Zoom and phone calls, it is important for me to be consistent and transparent with them when they hear from me.

Trust is critically important. Without trust and mutual respect during times of uncertainly, any communication becomes ineffective and unsettling.

Trust can be fortified my making yourself available on a regular basis during challenging times and being transparent in every communication.

Leadership roles in college athletics are often demanding and stressful. Describe activities you have incorporated to maintain self-care. Routines? Personal Time Away? Physical Activities?

I do my best to go for a run every morning after engaging in some quite time.

Loss and defeat are just as much a part of leadership as winning and overcoming. Like cheering and celebration come with the wins, so do tears and grief with loss. In general, how do you process grief? How do you process loss? Describe a defining moment in your career where one or both were a necessary part of your journey as a leader.

I process grief and loss as experiences along my journey that allows for growth opportunities. In my role as vice president for intercollegiate athletics, I am keenly aware that my job title is separate from my identity. My responsibility as a husband and father is paramount and any professional accomplishment pales in comparison to what it means to me to excel in my responsibilities in caring for and nurturing my family.

Featured Leadership – Leading in the Unknown 2020

**Earl Edwards, Director of Athletics
University of California – San Diego**

How do you define excellence in this season of the unknown?

>Clearly in this period it's about more than just game and competition.

>It's about ensuring that this period is a laboratory for personal development. This is a time when we must go deep with the relationships with our student-athletes. It's not just about academics, it about holistic development, particularly in the realm of decision-making. Student-athletes have more liberties and a voice more than ever.

>Excellence now is also about how athletics can unify campus, engage alumni, inspire the community, and "tell our story." Controlling our narrative is vital and we have devoted significant personnel and resources around this effort.

How have your core values changed, remained the same, or evolved?

>It comes down to integrity and resilience. This is a time when our core values are tested. It's also a time to best

teach our student-athletes how to apply core values, particularly resilience. How to make the right choices, how to stay prepared when the competition schedule has been altered, how to maintain focus in the classroom, and how to serve others during a national pandemic. It's important that our young people are pushed and understand that the bar is still high.

What do you think the future of social justice is in college athletics?

I feel the future is bright. College athletics is a great platform for society to follow. We have made significant strides... recognizing the importance of Juneteenth, making voting a priority, and educating around it.

We must keep the dialogue going in all spaces in our business. This is a time to empower student-athletes to have a voice, to influence policy, to have discourse around having a respect for difference, and to identify our leaders for future generations.

How has your communication style changed, remained the same, or stayed the same?

Being visible despite the issues of in-person meetings is important. In this period, staff, coaches, and

> student-athletes need to know that you are engaged and that you care about their well-being. I've learned to use Zoom to my advantage… I have more touches with my team, and they all know that I'm a call or Zoom meeting away. This definitely has been a "high-touch" opportunity for me to reaffirm everything that we stand for and despite the obvious challenges, we will not compromise our integrity.

Featured Leadership – Leading in the Unknown 2020

Tom Douple, Commissioner
The Summit League – NCAA Division I Intercollegiate Athletic Conference

How would you define this moment of the unknown?

I have never seen anything like this in my 44 years of being in this business. We have a confluence of things coming together at once... issues surrounding Name, Image, and Likeness; Social Justice; COVID-19. It mirrors what's going on in our society.

How do you define excellence in this season of the unknown?

I think it's about being diligent in trying to find the answers to the unknown questions.

We have imperfect solutions to unknown problems.

I focus on making the best decisions for our membership daily, particularly for our student-athletes. They have been impacted the most in this period.

How have your core values changed, remained the same, or been elevated during this period?

My values have been tested. However, I've remained focused on the well-being of our student-athletes.

One of the core values that I've really focused on is accountability. It important for me to be accountable for the Summit League Conference staff, our conference board of directors, our student-athletes, and coaches and staff members across our conference. Being accountable means that I remain steady in my decision-making and not make knee jerk decisions that in this challenging period could be fatal.

How have you added value in this challenging time of leadership?

I bring 44 years of experience to the table... I've added value to my team by being patient and offering constructive criticism when things are not executed perfectly. I don't believe this is a period where leaders need to focus on perfection, instead the effort and energy needs to be on making sure the ball is moving down the field. There is nothing wrong with focusing on first downs instead of touchdowns.

What is the future of social justice in our industry?

Our issues surrounding social justice has brought forth the voice of our student-athletes. Our business is truly a melting pot for our student-athletes. To some degree, society needs to take lessons from our industry. We have come together quickly and have elevated the student-athlete voice and prioritized a respect for difference. I go back to a statement Jesse Jackson made years ago at a dinner I attended. He said, "We don't need more police, we need more coaches for our youth." I think this is the right approach we need for our country.

How have you prioritized self-care during this period?

Honestly, I have not done a good job at all. I stress eat more than I should and need to incorporate exercise into my daily routine.

Spending time with my grandchildren has been my therapy. When I'm with them, I'm able to be in the moment and forget about the pressing issues of the day.

Featured Leadership – Leading in the Unknown 2020

Trev Alberts, Vice Chancellor/ Director of Athletics University of Nebraska Omaha

How would you define excellence in this season?

> I think it's a matter of defining what Utopia looks like...
>
> Excellence in this season is all about being transparent to our student-athletes, coaches, and staff. Encouraging them not to be paralyzed by fear, not to capitulate to the virus.
>
> You cannot be excellent during these times if you are not over-communicating. As a former football player, I believe more than ever this is a time when everyone in the organization must know the play that needs to be executed.

How have your core values changes, remained the same, or evolved?

> This period of uncertainty has reminded us of what we stand for... our values at Omaha are non-negotiable. If anything, are core values have been communicated and exemplified on a higher level.
>
> Honestly, this is far from the days when I first started as AD at Omaha. I've evolved from a soloist to a

conductor now... much more collaborative, engaging more stakeholders, and more open all the voices at the table.

How has your communication style changed, remained the same, or evolved?

I'm definitely more aware of how I communicate. Emails can be misunderstood and are impersonal... so I've been better at slowing down and picking up the phone or scheduling a quick Zoom call instead of sending out countless emails to staff and coaches.

I've also been intentional about making sure that directives, deadlines, and priorities are clear and understood. There are so many more moving pieces happening now than before. Coaches and staff are anxious. It's important that despite all of this they are clear on expectations and our vision moving forward.

In your opinion, what is the future of social justice in college athletics?

We have adopted an "everyone for everyone" campaign at Omaha. This is a great time for storytelling that underscores unity, collaboration, equality, teamwork... all things that are important for our industry.

> It's amazing what happens when we all just sit down and talk. What we discover is that we are a lot more alike than we think. This can only happen if we are secure in ourselves.
>
> ***How have you prioritized self-care in this challenging period?***
>
> I have done a fairly good job of keeping myself together. I'm on the treadmill most days and lift weight 4-5 days a week. It's challenging some days, because our jobs are so much more emotionally draining. We don't know what to expect on a daily basis.

Featured Leadership – Leading in the Unknown 2020

David Harris, Director of Athletics
University of Northern Iowa

As a Division I Athletics Director, how did you know this moment (this season) was different?

I knew it was serious when competitions started to get canceled, when we had to work remotely and vacate campus. In Iowa, it can be 25 degrees below 0 and campus will still be open. When we were instructed to go home, I knew this was something that would plague us for a while. I knew that this would be a moment of major adjustment and resolve.

How would you define excellence in this season of the unknown?

I think this is a time where leaders must be able to anticipate, plan, provide structure, and make appropriate decisions based on personnel.

Leaders must be able to "look around the corner" (see what everyone can't see) and be able to anticipate issues relating to student-athlete welfare, managing coaches, providing perspective around Name, Image, and Likeness (NIL).

As the leader of your Athletics Department, how have your core values changed, remained the same, or been fortified?

> I've been tested for sure, but my core values have remained the same. I have been disciplined and self-aware enough to not change due to the dire circumstances. I'm focused on what is in the best interest of the long-term growth and development of the department. Yes, I've had to make short-term decisions related to loss of revenue, staffing, possible sport elimination... but I've stayed true to making decisions that are at the core focused on the welfare of our student-athletes.

How do you feel you have added value during this period of the unknown?

> I have added value by providing a sense of calm during turbulence... I've been poised, firm in my decision-making, and utilizing a high level of discernment. I've been intentional about getting people to be more collaborative... not to work in silos or isolation. In that sense it's really improved our department.
>
> I've added value for my president by providing the "real" view of what's the state of our department. I've done a good job of describing a plan on how we

will get through the storm, best serve our student-athletes, and remain connected to our fans.

In your opinion, how do you think social justice will continue to play out in our industry?

I believe it will head in a positive direction... I'm optimistic. However, I think there is still much work to do from a structural and planning standpoint where we get beyond emotion. We will need strong leaders to emerge... and those leaders will likely be the student-athletes we are serving now.

This should not be seasonal, we need social justice to be a priority not only for college athletics, but higher education at large. There is no better time to highlight this point.

How have you maintained self-care in this unstable period?

Honestly, it's been up and down... the emotional stress has caused me to back off a bit. I just don't have the energy. Self-care for me has been prioritizing time with my family first thing in the morning.

I've focused my self-care on love rather than my physical well-being...

Featured Leadership – Leading in the Unknown 2020

Bob Bowlsby, Commissioner
Big XII Conference

How would you define excellence in this period of the unknown?

Excellence clearly has a different definition in this period of turbulence. Excellence will emerge from the people who are the most disciplined. Disciplined in their thoughts, disciplined in their execution, disciplined in the way they serve others.

The bar for excellence is lower, particularly in what we are seeing in competition. The level of play is lower, conditioning is suffering, and the ability to be consistent has been disrupted.

How have your core values changed, remained the same, and/or been elevated?

I've relied the most on my core values in this period. I can't emphasize enough the value of discipline during this pandemic. I've been very deliberate and methodical in my decision-making... all the way from the way that I lead my family to the way that I lead and govern the conference.

Patience has been the key. This is not a time when you want to rush decisions and pressure your staff to execute, because there is no precedent for what we are dealing with. We have been forced to rely on fluidity more than any time in our industry's existence.

How has your communication style changed, altered, or remained the same?

I've been more intentional with my communication. For years, I've enjoyed managing by walking around... sitting in someone's office and gaining an understanding of how they think and solve problems, getting a sense of the vision they have for the conference, and getting a better sense of their strengths and opportunities for growth.

I've definitely done a better job of communicating "down the chain" of command in our office. With the convenience of Zoom, I'm able to over-communicate and provide information to staff more efficiently. This has eased some of the anxiety and fears of the staff.

In this period, I have also prioritized cross-pollination within our office and conference leadership. Although we are still in a precarious position of the unknown, we have done a good job of understanding our challenges, opportunities, and threats to our league.

What is the future of social justice in college athletics?

I'm disappointed that we haven't made more progress. Unfortunately, we have received negative feedback about blending politics and sports. I encourage our student-athletes to have a voice and express their inner-most feelings and thoughts about race, discrimination, and equality.

I believe college athletics can be a beacon for our society…

It's time for people of color to be hired versus just interviewed.

What is your perspective of self-care in this trying period?

Believe it or not, I have not lived in my home for months. My wife and I are getting some work done on our house and I've been sheltered in the local Residence Inn. I've eaten too much junk food. I try to take long walks and bike rides when I can, but it's not nearly enough.

I've focused my self-care on love rather than my physical well-being.

Featured Leadership – Leading in the Unknown 2020

Tim Duncan, Vice President/ Director of Athletics & Recreation
University of New Orleans

How would you define excellence in this season of the unknown?

> There is no playbook for this... excellence is in how we communicate with each other, how we position our student-athletes for success... how we explain the future ahead (i.e., strategic informational sessions to coaches, staff, student-athletes).
>
> "There is not one of us that's not smarter than all of us."

How have your core values changed, remained the same, or grown in this period of the unknown?

> If anything, my core values as a leader have been elevated and even more clarified. I have heightened my communication around teamwork, accessibility, and service...
>
> I've also placed a high premium on judgement in this period. The business of college athletics is all about having the right judgement on hiring, positioning staff for success, managing stakeholders, and decisions on

how to stay relevant in an unprecedented time in our industry and nation.

How has your communication style changed or remained the same during crises?

I'm an extrovert by nature, so I felt the need to over-communicate to my team... making sure everyone is on the same page. I feel I have gone the "extra mile" to let my team know that I care about them beyond what they can do for UNO Athletics. I empathize how this has impacted them personally as well as their families.

Without the proper and timely communication, our department cannot execute the agreed upon goals that our department has committed to... this is the true test of our commitment.

How have you added value during this period?

Again, I over-communicate... even to my president. I provide perspective and lay out clearly the challenges and opportunities.

I also add value by providing each person on my executive team a voice... we make collaborative decisions regarding the strategic direction of our department. This gives them a real sense of empowerment and ownership of where we are going.

I've also added value by communicating frequently with my student-athletes. I want to provide as much comfort as possible and let them know that I'm accessible to them. This has been helpful in allowing them a space to feel vulnerable about their fears, anxieties, and expectations of our department.

How do you feel social justice will continue to play out in college athletics?

I think it's clear that issues surrounding social injustice is here to stay... and our student-athletes are a huge part of that. Our platform of college athletics is a huge platform to make change in the larger society. There is so much positive that we can do in our industry to make a change. We just need to do our part in sustaining this effort.

How have you maintained self-care during this turbulent season?

I take long walks with my family. I read and listen to audio books at night to bring me down from my stressful days.

My Concluding Thought

This book has been a passion project that emerged as societal challenges continue to mount across the intercollegiate athletics context. As I embraced the challenges by deepening my values, I became reflective on the need to have a new framework for leading into the unknown. This book represents a new paradigm and direction for leaders who seek to embrace a culturally relevant style of leadership. The leaders who have generously offered their experiences and voices to this work have been invaluable in helping me articulate a new paradigm for leadership. This book represents the collective experiences and wisdom as well as new leadership strategies that constitute a new *playbook* for how to lead into the unknown. The expectation is utilizing this playbook will yield wins for intercollegiate athletics broadly, and specifically your institution. I will forever be thankful to the leaders who devoted the time, especially in these uncertain days, to make a difference for this project and future generations who may be faced with tremendous uncertainties in the future. I am both grateful and honored to offer a timely contribution to not only intercollegiate athletics, but higher education at large.

References

Bell, Derrick. (2003). *Ethical Ambition: Living a Life of Meaning and Worth*. Bloomsbury.

Browne, A. J., Varcoe, C., Smye, V., Reimer-Kirkham, S., Lynam, M. J., & Wong, S. (2009). Cultural safety and the challenges of translating critically oriented knowledge in practice. *Nursing philosophy: an international journal for healthcare professionals*, *10*(3), 167–179. https://doi.org/10.1111/j.1466-769X.2009.00406.x

Caligiuri, P., & Lundby, K. (2014). *Developing Cross-Cultural Competencies Through Global Teams*. (pp. 123-139). Springer New York.

Dimitriadis, V. D., & Pistikopoulos, E. N. (1995). Flexibility analysis of dynamic systems. *Industrial & Engineering Chemistry Research, 34*(12), 4451-4462. doi:10.1021/ie00039a036

Ehrlich, J. (2017). Mindful leadership. *Organizational Dynamics*, 46(4), 233-243. https://doi.org/10.1016/j.orgdyn.2017.05.002

Fox, C., Davis, P., & Baucus, M. (2020). Corporate social responsibility during unprecedented crises: The role of authentic leadership and business model flexibility. *Management Decision,* doi:10.1108/MD-08-2020-1073

Franco, A. R., Vieira, R. M., Riegel, F., & Oliveira Crossetti, Maria da Graca. (2019). Steering clear from 'lost in translation': Cross-cultural translation, adaptation, and validation of critical thinking mindset self-rating form to university students. *Studies in Higher Education* (Dorchester-on-Thames), 1-11.

George, B., & Bennis, W. G. (2009). *7 Lessons for Leading in Crisis*. Jossey-Bass, San Francisco.

Greenleaf, R. K., & Spears, L. C. (2002). *Servant Leadership: A Journey into the Nature of Legitimate Power and Greatness*. Paulist Press.

Heath, D., & Heath, C. (2019). *The Power of Moments*. Random House UK.

Hedrick, A. (2000). Dynamic flexibility training. *Strength and Conditioning Journal*, 22(5), 33.

Hunter, J. C. (2012). *The Servant: A Simple Story about the True Essence of Leadership*. Crown Business, Crown Publishing Group, New York.

King, M. L. (1963). *Strength to love*. Hodder and Stoughton.

Kouzes, J. M., & Posner, B. Z. (2016). *Learning Leadership: The Five Fundamentals of*

Becoming an Exemplary Leader. The Leadership Challenge, San Francisco.

Koyenikan, I. (2016). *Wealth for All: Living a Life of Success at the Edge of Your Ability*. Grandeur Touch, LLC.

Krebs, R. J. (2009). Bronfenbrenner's bioecological theory of human development and the process of development of sports talent. *International Journal of Sport Psychology, 40*(1), 108-135.

Luke, J. S. (1998). *Catalytic Leadership: Strategies for an Interconnected World*. Jossey-Bass, San Francisco.

Maxwell, J. C. (2014). *15 Invaluable Laws of Growth: Live Them and Reach Your Potential*. Center Street, Hachette Book Group, New York.

Maxwell, J. C. (2017). *Intentional Living: Choosing a Life that Matters*. Center Street, Hachette Book Group, New York.

Merriam-Webster. (n.d.). Catalyst. In *Meriam-Webster.com dictionary*. https://www.merriam-webster.com/dictionary/catalyst

Validation (n. d.). *Dictionary.com unabridged*. http://www.dictionary.com/browse/validation?s=t

Wicks, R. J. (2012). *Riding the Dragon: 10 Lessons for Inner Strength in*

Challenging Times. Notre Dame, IN: Sorin Books.

About The Author

Dr. Brandon E. Martin is the Vice Chancellor/Director of Athletics at the University of Missouri—Kansas City. Martin brings over two decades of experience within higher education as a former student-athlete, athletics administrator, and educator. Dr. Martin serves as an Executive in Residence in the UMKC School of Education and Applied Behavioral Sciences; the Henry Bloch School of Management; and Race, Ethnic, and Gender Studies. Dr. Martin is the Co-Chair of the Black Athletic Director Alliance, and a Board Member of the Kansas City Sports Commission. Martin is a proud member of Kappa Alpha Psi Fraternity Inc. and Sigma Pi Phi Fraternity.

www.ingramcontent.com/pod-product-compliance
Lightning Source LLC
Chambersburg PA
CBHW070550010526
44118CB00012B/1281